STARTING YOUR CAREER AS AN

INTERIOR DESIGNER

STARTING YOUR CAREER AS AN

INTERIOR DESIGNER

ROBERT K. HALE & THOMAS L. WILLIAMS
WRITTEN WITH MURPHY HOOKER

ALLWORTH PRESS
NEW YORK

14   13   12   11   10   6   5   4   3   2

Published by Allworth Press
An imprint of Allworth Communications, Inc.
10 East 23rd Street, New York, NY 10010

Cover design by Derek Bacchus
Interior design by The Roberts Group
Page composition/typography by Integra Software Services, Pvt., Ltd., Pondicherry, India
Cover photo by Joel Puliatti

ISBN-13: 978-1-58115-659-1

Library of Congress Cataloging-in-Publication Data:
Hale, Robert K.
    Starting your career as an interior designer / by Robert K. Hale and Thomas L. Williams.
        p. cm.
    ISBN 978-1-58115-659-1
    1. Interior decoration— Vocational guidance.   I. Williams, Thomas L., 1949-   II. Title.

NK2116.H34 2009
747.092—dc22

                                                                                2008041105

Printed in the United States of America

DEDICATED TO NORMA C. WILLIAMS

*Loving mother and
pioneering, entrepreneurial businesswoman*

CONTENTS

FOREWORD

Since you purchased this book, I can only assume that you want either to become an interior designer or to become a more successful one. In either case, it is clear that in *Starting Your Career as an Interior Designer*, you have found a resource of unprecedented value.

For over twenty years, I have studied the competitive nature of industries and taught entrepreneurship at the University of Texas at Austin. I have looked at fields as diverse as software, manufacturing, and retail. When, some years ago, I was presented with the opportunity to study the interior design industry, I came away with an unexpected, and as of yet unaltered, opinion: Interior design is the most complex industry I have ever seen.

I have often described being an interior designer as tantamount to trying to run a law firm (detail-oriented with a time-billing mentality), a construction firm (intricate coordination of people, places, and things to complete a job), and a group therapy session (keeping clients happy) ... all at the same time!

Intrigued, I expanded my field of research and discovered an even more astonishing fact—the virtual absence of business education available for professionals in this challenging field. I found that the gap between the creative skills that are often innate and the business skills that must be learned is greater than in any other industry I have studied. This gap has only increased over the past five years as the challenges facing interior designers have grown more daunting, driven by forces that strategic planners would term "creative destruction" and "collapsing value chains."

What this means to you is that the path to your profitability in the future will be very different from the one traveled by other designers in the past. You will need very different skills. The industry is being shaken by powerful forces, including the Internet, megastores, do-it-yourselfers, and a plethora of design magazines and television shows. You will have to know how to capitalize on these trends rather than be victimized by them.

Everyone, it seems, wants to be a designer today, which is somewhat surprising considering the challenges designers face. To be blunt, few are able to earn and sustain a good living. But there are factors that highly successful designers share. There are driving philosophies and core business practices that can dramatically boost your chances of success. And, fortunately for you, hundreds of these factors are contained in the pages of this landmark book.

In *Starting Your Career as an Interior Designer*, Robert K. Hale and Thomas L. Williams have done a masterful job of never shying away from the complexity of which I speak. Yet rather than succumb to the temptation of offering simple solutions, they put forward an array of strategic alternatives for you to choose from. Where necessary, they give full voice to opposing points of view. Skilled designers themselves, Hale and Williams go into great detail about the factors that determine a designer's ability to remain viable—factors like competition and pricing wars, and even licensing and accreditation.

The bite-sized nuggets presented in each chapter, along with interspersed case studies in the voices of other designers, are just two of the many structural components that keep the pages of this book turning. It is anything but a boring business tome.

The authors describe the profession of interior design as an "adventure," and the same could be said for reading this book. It is infused with an inspiring voice—*you can do it*—yet steeped in the business realities that the authors' distinguished careers have provided.

Starting Your Career as an Interior Designer is destined to become a perennial book that designers and would-be designers will read for years to come, even as the industry continues its rapid transition.

In all critical areas, from the niche markets you may want to consider to the nature of competition and pricing, the authors have drawn not only on their combined fifty-plus years of experience, but also on their extensive research. This book is comprehensive in scope, yet echoing beyond the scholarship one hears the voices of the authors like those of a best friend and mentor. Hale and Williams—two proven professionals—take less experienced designers by the hand, whisper sage counsel in their ears, and give them the courage and the confidence to go forward on their own.

The authors have been through the design wars and have not just seen, but have *experienced*, the wrenching changes of an industry in transition. They have adapted, and despite the award-winning design work of their own creation, one can't help but wonder if this book won't be their ultimate legacy to the world of interior design. While others might write books about color, form, or function, Hale and Williams have gone to the very heart of the future of design: If its practitioners can't manage the complexity of the business side of things, they will not have the time or the financial resources to express their creative artistry. The result will be a sea of corporate, cookie-cutter design commodities masquerading as art.

So yes, this is a book for artists, but also for realists. It is a book for those who want to see life as an adventure and work as fulfilling. It is for those who, one hopes, will be able to face their future challenges with the same grace, intelligence, and humor as have Hale and Williams.

As one who has come to respect and admire the enormous entrepreneurial vigor of the professional interior designers in this country, I heave a huge sigh of relief, confident that this book will play a vital role in keeping that flow of talent alive and on track for many years to come.

David P. Shepherd, University of Texas at Austin

INTRODUCTION

A re you coming to the interior design game later than most? Are you considered by some to be a late bloomer? It's okay; you can confide in Hale-Williams. We won't tell. We know it's crass to ask one's age in real life, but as your career doctors, we need to know. You're how old? Jokes aside, we know many of our readers are not fresh-faced young design graduates; some of you are thirty- or forty-year-old novices who never attended a four-year design college. Perhaps you're at a point in your life at which you're considering changing vocations or reentering the work force after taking time off. We may, from time to time, refer to you all as neophyte designers, young designers, or even whippersnappers. Whatever the word choice, understand that we mean all of you coming into the industry for the first time.

Regardless of your story, you're here because you want to learn more about the "business" of interior design. If you fit the late-bloomer profile, that's great. Be proud and stay motivated. There is no shame in changing career tracks mid stream. It's actually quite common in the design world.

Some of the most talented designers working today literally stumbled on their passion for design. Over the years, we have met many wonderful young designers who were interested in owning and operating a design business but had no idea how to get started. Sure, design schools teach you how to master design elements like pattern, space, and color, but what about opening a studio, balancing a budget, or managing a tough client?

We concluded that there simply weren't enough books or classes offered (anywhere) that deal with the "business" of interior design. Today students who gravitate to design from other careers must fend for themselves. What a shame, we thought, so we decided to write a business-savvy book for the new generation of design entrepreneurs—introducing *Starting Your Career as an Interior Designer*.

What makes us qualified to mentor? Hale-Williams Interior Design has been in the luxury residential interior design business for over thirty years. In addition, for the last seven years, one of us (Tom) has taught a business practices course for the interior design program at Monterey Peninsula College. Along the way, we think we've learned a few things about running a successful interior design firm that will help you get started.

Certainly, the art of interior design is what drew us to the profession, but it's the business that has kept us in the game for all this time. Just like most of you, we had to earn a living from day one and never had the luxury of letting one or two jobs a year cover our costs. We expect each and every project to successfully create a profit for our firm and a salary for us. You should, too.

Dive in—you'll find *Starting Your Career as an Interior Designer* will help you understand the fundamentals of the design business. You'll learn how to:

- Understand design segments
- Build a business plan
- Set up your own design studio
- Research your target market
- Market yourself and your business
- Attract the right type of client
- Understand business models
- Write contracts and letters of agreement
- Run your operation
- Network and advertise
- Sell yourself to the design world
- Understand pricing and fees
- Capitalize on buzz and word of mouth
- Develop a network of business allies
- Hone your presentation techniques
- Manage clients
- Budget projects
- Set goals and improve your bottom line

...and much more. Becoming an interior designer is not easy; it requires a dedication not found in many professions. Becoming a successful entrepreneur requires even more hard work. You need a solid grounding in all aspects of interior design, but even more, you must have an unbending desire to succeed. We can't make you want it more than your competition, but we can show you that a successful interior design firm is based, first and foremost, on sound business practices. It is these valuable business practices that we want to share with you.

Just remember, no one will show you the "yellow brick road" to success. Be prepared to pave your own road to glory. That's what we did. To some this may sound daunting, while to others, the limitless possibility of designing your own career path from its foundation is a thrilling prospect. For those who are currently feeling that tingly, tantalizing entrepreneurial sensation, this book is for you.

STARTING YOUR CAREER AS AN

INTERIOR DESIGNER

CHAPTER 1

DESIGNS ON AN INDUSTRY

It's Not a Job, It's an Adventure

> "Destiny is not a matter of chance;
> it is a matter of choice.
> It is not a thing to be waited for;
> it is a thing to be achieved."
> —WILLIAM JENNINGS BRYAN

When we began flirting with the idea of writing a design book, the first question we asked ourselves was whether or not we had anything startlingly new to say about operating a successful design business that hadn't been said before (ad nauseam). Neither of us had any desire to write yet another bone-dry design textbook that readers typically dread, skim, and then forget; nor were we interested in condensing our life's work into a CliffsNotes guide on interior design for students with Attention Deficit Disorder, so we decided to write a book that essentially acts as a "paperback" mentor for young design professionals who, we believe, must not only understand the fundamentals in order to succeed, but must also develop agile business minds to go with their creative designer souls. To be sure, neophytes, it won't just happen overnight. You have to make your destiny come to you.

But isn't interior design a creative calling? Yes, indeed. However, like many artists, most interior designers starting out fail to grasp the obvious fact that interior design is a business and that, regardless of how much creative talent you have, if you aren't skilled in the art of commerce, you're going to crash and burn.

So, for the sake of simplicity, we're going to assume all of our readers are talented "creative designers" and focus our attention on the other essential parts of the design business that will go a long way toward determining your professional success. A good sign for you, and for your career,

3

is your savvy choice to buy this book. We think you'll find it full of lessons on the business fundamentals as well as healthy doses of reality and inspirational supplements for novice designers interested in building on their education and eventually starting their own interior design firms.

So dive in, have fun, and learn how to innovate, adapt, and prosper as an interior design entrepreneur without selling your soul or losing the farm.

BIRTH OF THE COOL

We aren't going to get into a comprehensive account of the evolution of the industry, but we do feel it's important to highlight some essential moments in design history so you aren't left entirely speechless when a wise guy at a cocktail party tries to flummox you with the question, "So, who was the first interior designer, anyway??"

In the Beginning

For all intents and purposes, modern interior design emerged out of the eighteenth century in Western Europe, specifically in London, Paris, and Florence, where design work was primarily overseen by upholsterers who sold furniture and fabrics and architects who employed artisans to complete their design schemes. Some of the craftsmen on the job were:

- Painters
- Builders
- Sculptors
- Upholsterers
- Cabinet makers
- Drapery makers
- Shopkeepers
- Antiquarians

A few of the dustier design tomes credit English architect and furniture designer William Kent as the first person to design an entire interior space, while others cite neoclassical architect Robert Adam as the best-known example of an architect who designed entire interiors "down to the doorknobs and fire-irons."

Society Dames Lead the American Revolution

Beginning in the late nineteenth century, interior design was considered a genteel art form plied by groups of society women, or well-heeled "ladies with taste," who weren't in it for the money but, rather, because they loved designing interior spaces.

By far the most famous of the pioneering socialite decorators was afflu-ent amateur Elsie de Wolfe, also known as Lady Mendl (1865–1950). A prominent figure in the society scenes of New York, London, and Paris, de Wolfe is credited as the first female professional decorator in the United States. Her early success proved to the predominantly male design com-munity that interior decorating could be a profession in which a woman's presence would not offend respectability.

A self-proclaimed "rebel in an ugly world," de Wolfe authored the 1913 book *The House in Good Taste* and became a legend in her own time by garnering the adoration of the world media. A skillful, self-promoting innovator, Lady Mendl was also very good at her job. She helped update the design of high-end homes from darker Victorian styles to fresher designs that featured soft colors and eighteenth-century French furniture. Among her elite residential clients were families like the Vanderbilts and the Duke and Duchess of Windsor.

De Wolfe also notably decorated interiors for the Colony Club and for what is now the Frick Museum in New York, all before World War I. Thanks in large part to Lady Mendl, the word "decorator" came into existence and the art of interior design began drawing the interest of the mainstream public.

Eleanor McMillen Brown was one of the most influential early inte-rior designers as well as a serious presence in New York's high society scene. She was also a serious professional. Brown founded the legend-ary design firm McMillen, Inc. in 1924, and then ran it for nearly six decades. In that time, her firm never strayed from the McMillen style: a reassuring traditionalism with a contemporary flair and feminine look that still has an enormous appeal to owners of rambling summer cottages in Southampton. To this day, McMillen, Inc. remains one of the best, most professional interior design firms in the country.

Another socially connected "lady" designer from New York and Philadelphia's elite set, Dorothy Draper, will forever be remembered for her use of large floral prints on fabrics and paper. Founder of Dorothy Draper Design, she was a master at using oversized furniture that was custom-built for a specific area. Draper did her part to help bring America out of the doldrums of the Depression and World War II by using bright colors and large-scale items to remodel commercial spaces like the Greenbrier Resort in West Virginia.

Other Pioneering Superstars

Of course, for decorators who needed the money, making a living from interior design didn't begin to factor into the equation until the moniker "interior designer" grew out of the fashionable world of the socialite deco-rator and ran into the bloodstream of the American popular culture.

In the early part of the twentieth century, aspiring designers on the outside of the society scenes in New York, London, and Paris saw the public's growing interest in design as an opportunity to make a living doing what they loved. Scores of young designers, like you, leapt at the chance.

Soon, the American public began to see work from a diverse cast of trendsetting "superstar" interior decorators who established their names on talent alone and had few society connections or little formal design education. Some of the notable pioneers in the field are mentioned below.

Syrie Maugham introduced the "white look" to American design in the early 1920s and, like many designers of her time, kept a shop and sold goods as well as her design services. Maugham was an excellent mentor to a number of designers and is still remembered today for the style and wit she employed in her designs.

Rose Cumming, an Australian who came to America during World War I, was another talent who demonstrated that women could be very successful interior designers. A self-described shopkeeper at heart, Cumming enjoyed the idea of never knowing who might walk through her shop door with a new challenge, work of art, or project. The creator of many memorable fabrics and wall coverings, many of which designers still use to this day, Cumming was mentored by famed New York decorator Mary Buel and drew from that experience to create one of the best-known brands in interior design.

Michael Taylor was another great example of an interior designer with superb branding skills, and was a revolutionary whose influence helped shape a new generation of design artists. Formally trained in San Francisco, Michael was one of a group of young designers who came out of interior design schools just after World War II. The founder of Michael Taylor Designs in 1985, he was the first to bring natural materials like concrete, wicker, and timber in from the outdoors and did more for the "white room" than any designer since Elsie de Wolfe or Syrie Maugham. Before his death in 1986, Taylor's over-scaled furniture designs had become virtually synonymous with the California lifestyle.

The career of one of our all-time favorite "gentleman" designers, Mark Hampton, is a study in diversity. Yet another excellent branding success story, Hampton was a student at the London School of Economics before switching gears to earn a master's degree in fine arts from New York University. With a thoughtful and educated design style, Hampton began his career with David Hicks in London and then returned to New York to work with the design firm McMillen, Inc. Hampton eventually created his own design house, Mark Hampton, LLC, and is known for his design vocabulary, which uses color, print, and luxury finishes to create clean interior designs. His book, *Mark Hampton on Decorating*, is a must-read for any student of interior design.

Department Store Divas

As is the case with any "start-up" profession, most U.S. designers coming out of the early modern era never achieved superstar status, but some were still able to make a living doing what they loved.

One tier of the modern design community got its start designing homes for the clients of large upscale department stores like Bloomingdale's, Harrods, Harvey Nichols, Sloans, and Liberty of London. These early department store designers made a nice living designing homes using in-house furnishings, fabrics, and accessories to create residential interiors that embodied the styles of their department stores and had that "Bloomingdale's" or "Liberty" look.

The Retail Designer Cometh

Despite all the efforts of our pioneering forefathers (and fabulous foremothers), most interior designers in the middle part of the twentieth century found trailblazing to be tough going, especially on their bottom line. Unless you were a socialite decorator, a superstar in the field, or a department store designer, few were paid well enough to make a living strictly on their "art."

An enterprising solution to the modern problem of "how to make money doing what you love" was to supplement one's creative passion by starting hybrid businesses, where designers owned and operated retail spaces while offering free design services to their clientele. Following in the footsteps of Rose Cumming and Syrie Maugham, designers who embraced the model of the retail merchant/interior designer found they were able to support their passion for design by procuring inventory (for clients) through wholesale distributors in large metropolitan area design centers.

Take a look around one of today's design meccas (London, New York, Paris, Milan, Hong Kong) and you'll notice these pioneer retail designers carved out a prosperous segment of the industry that still thrives today. But if you ask the opinion of a "superstar" or "pure designer," you'll find that some take issue with their retail brethren's hybrid business model. Why?

Because some "pure designers" don't believe designers should be earning the bulk of their income as merchants or salespeople. Ask us, and we'll tell you it doesn't matter how you do it, just as long as you do it.

Furniture Boom

Socialite decorators, superstar designers, department store divas, and retail designers weren't the only design games in town in the middle part of the twentieth century; yet another business model materialized just in time to play a key role in the interior design boom of the 1950s. Large furniture chains like Ethan Allen capitalized on the growing public demand for custom home furnishings by opening stores around the country. Their timing could not have been better.

Like their booming department store competitors, custom furniture stores played a key role in the advancement of the designer cause by minting yet another new job title for young decorators: the furniture store designer. To this day, these in-house interior stylists assist clients with the purchasing, design, and placement of customizable interior furnishings for homes and offices.

Try socializing with a few furniture store designers and you'll find that most aren't (yet) the high-end design divas they always aspired to be, but they're still artists pursuing their dreams while making a buck and satisfying a huge consumer demand.

Like Jazz, an American Art

Though practiced all over the world for some three hundred years, many consider the rise of the modern interior designer to be, like jazz, a fundamentally American creation. Some historians attribute this rise to the favorable times in which the American designer emerged and flourished, while others cite specific factors like:

- A humming economy after the end of World War II
- The thriving American media that exposed the impressionable masses to glamorous interior visions from superstar designers
- A never-before-seen baby boom from a war-torn nation of new couples
- A great family migration from the big cities to the suburbs
- The founding of professional interior design associations

Without a doubt, America helped to broaden greatly the appeal of interior design by taking it out of the realm of the elite and into the world of anyone who could afford it. As an American art form, it empowered many designers to create styles for a much wider audience than ever before. This was not so in the rest of the world.

Finally, one can't disregard the impact of the "domestic decade" (the 1950s) on the modern design boom. Who was going to decorate all those new family homes in the suburbs? You guessed it: a new generation of interior designers.

EARLY CAREER TRACKS

Believe it or not, although some designers were earning fine arts degrees, the study of interior design was, for years, taught through the home economics department. To this day, some design degrees are still obtained under the home economics umbrella. If you find that to be an archaic pairing, you're not alone.

To whom do you think a home economics degree is directed? To Sally Homemaker, of course. Not that there is anything wrong with being a domestic goddess, but we strongly believe interior design is an art and a business; it really hasn't much to do with building and maintaining a functional family home.

How many men in the 1950s were eager to earn design degrees from a home economics department? Some did, actually, but most learned their trade not by going to school but by joining design firms and becoming design assistants, then junior designers. Revered modern designers like Billy Baldwin and Carlton Varney bypassed formal training to learn the trade in the trenches by apprenticing under some of the best in the business (Rose Cumming and Dorothy Draper). So which is the better career track—school or experience?

A four-year bachelor of science or bachelor of fine arts degree in interior design will certainly be helpful in your career, but remember: Some of the most successful designers in the world never earned degrees. Some of us are born naturals, while others have degrees in other fields and use that experience to run our design businesses.

Despite what many professional organizations would have you believe, a degree does not automatically make you a successful interior designer, nor does the lack of a degree condemn you to failure. The degree is not essential, but the education is, so work as an apprentice, study the industry, attend seminars, and use your time to self-educate. And repeat after us: It doesn't matter how you do it, just as long as you do it!

THE PROFESSIONAL ORGANIZATIONS

With the industry in full stride by the 1960s, some of the hottest interior designers had become brand names while others had become stars, and several were filthy rich. Designers steeped in pop culture made waves by producing innovative works that coolly reflected what was happening in the real world. After all these years, interior design was still in vogue.

But what finally cemented interior design (as a profession) in the world marketplace wasn't all the publicity, the innovative designs, or the sizzle; it was the formation of professional design associations. Established in part to overcome the stereotype that interior designers had a lack of organizational and business sense, professional design groups helped establish sound business practices in what was then still an unorganized art form.

Borrowing the Architects' Blueprint

By borrowing the blueprint from professional architecture groups, designers created organizational standards and workflows of their own. The first professional interior design organization was the American Institute of Decorators (AID), founded in 1931, which became the American Institute of Interior Designers (AIID) in 1961. The second major group was the National Society of Interior Designers (NSID), formed in 1957. The two merged in 1974 to create what is presently the largest organization of interior designers, the American Society of Interior Designers, or ASID.

Some of the key organizational functions and duties that ASID and other professional design groups have embedded permanently in the industry are:

- Organizing offices, which have had wildly varying methods of operation
- Fees and markup guidelines on the purchase of merchandise
- Operating methods based on basic business and accounting principles
- Systemized workflows to counter the dearth of business standards in the industry
- State licensing standards, which require ASID members to have design degrees and pass the National Comprehensive Interior Design Quiz (NCIDQ) for initiation
- Business tools such as letters of agreement and methods and practices for billing, purchasing, inventory, and budgeting
- Education on professionalism in the industry

Even more significant were professional design organizations (like ASID, International Interior Design Association, and International Furnishings and Design Association, to name a few) that forever changed the industry by introducing a new school method for charging clients, called transparent pricing, into the marketplace (see chapter 6, "Defining Your Dream").

Does Membership Matter?

As a young designer, you have probably heard how important membership in one of these professional organizations is, but is it really true? Do any of our clients really know what these organizations do for our business? We don't believe they do, nor do they care. Throughout our careers, we've asked clients for their opinions, and 99 percent cannot tell us what the acronyms stand for or represent. And why should they? The organizations, for the most part, have done a terrible job of marketing and public relations.

So why do designers join? In our opinion, it's peer pressure. The big three (ASID, IIDA, and IFDA) use fear tactics to persuade clients to work exclusively with their member designers. Their organizational stance is: If clients do not hire a "professionally certified" designer, the project is in utter jeopardy of failure and the job will not be up to local or national "professional" standards. We say that's ridiculous.

Take it from a couple of old pros: Don't buy what these organizations are selling until you decide exactly what you want from them. Their methods are just another protectionist approach to membership and another way to intimidate would-be clients.

Are members of these organizations better designers? It's difficult to gauge, as judgment of an interior designer's work is always subjective. That even applies to parts of the NCIDQ. Is it a fair and unbiased test of interior design skill and knowledge? Maybe, but that's a judgment call on the part of ASID.

The point is that nothing is objective in our world. There is no question that professionalism is important in our business; we just don't believe there are a few monolithic organizations that define what is "professional" in our world. The bottom line is: If you want to join a professional organization, go for it. But never, and we mean never, let them bully you into membership with fear tactics and intimidation. It's not worth it!

CASE STUDY: BILLY BALDWIN

"There is nothing quite so boring as false refinement,
or so vulgar as misplaced elegance."

—BILLY BALDWIN

Billy Baldwin, a legend in the field of modern interior design, believed the first rule of decorating is that you can break almost all of the other rules. Among the first to believe in an "American Look" for interior design, Baldwin is known for inventing the "Modern Continental" look in the 1940s and for helping to bring "clean" styles to the design of interiors.

Born in Baltimore, Maryland, in the early 1900s to a socially connected mother, Baldwin built a design career that spanned five decades. He attended a private prep school in Baltimore and then, for a short time, Princeton University. He left school to pursue his dreams in the real world—and why not? Baldwin was the quintessential "natural," one of the best at building phenomenal working relationships with his design mentors. After leaving Princeton, Baldwin met his first mentor, Mrs. John W. Garrett, wife of the U.S. ambassador and mistress of the famed Evergreen House in Baltimore. The Evergreen House was known for its beautiful design and vast collection of art, from original Picassos and Raoul Dufy watercolors to priceless Chinese furniture.

Garrett introduced Baldwin to scores of socially connected luminaries who helped further his career. Through his newfound connections, Baldwin secured his first major job working as an interior designer under Mrs. Thomas Symington. Known for her vast collection of Italian beds, Spanish chairs, and Portuguese tables, Symington gave Baldwin his first big break. As is the way with good publicity, Baldwin's work with Symington attracted the attention of his next major design mentor: Ruby Ross Wood of New York City.

The ghostwriter of Elsie de Wolfe's landmark design book, *The House in Good Taste*, Wood was Baldwin's most supportive design mentor. A notable design pioneer in her own right, Wood was the first woman to head an American department store's interior decoration department— the famous Au Quatrieme at Wanamaker's in New York.

Soon after Wood met Baldwin, she invited him to New York in 1935 to work for her company, Ruby Ross Wood, Inc. Of course, he accepted. Recognizing talent when she saw it, Wood took Baldwin under her wing and helped him launch the career that would define his life.

In later years, Baldwin often quoted from the breadth of lessons Wood taught him about interior design. Like all great mentors, she helped instill in Baldwin a design ethos that would stick for a lifetime.

Within a year of joining Ruby Ross Wood, Inc., Baldwin secured a commission that put him on the map. Baldwin found that, through excellent word of mouth, clients began asking for him by name. He ultimately left Ruby Ross Wood in 1950 to create his own New York design firm, Baldwin and Martin, where he was among the first to bring clean styles to interior design.

After achieving world fame, Billy Baldwin had the pleasure of designing for some of the most iconic figures in modern American history. He designed singer/songwriter Cole Porter's famous Waldorf-Astoria apartment, as well as residential spaces for Diana Vreeland of *Vogue* magazine and Mrs. William S. Paley, wife of the (then) president of CBS.

Baldwin's work could also be seen in the homes of two of the most mysterious style icons of the twentieth century—Jackie Kennedy Onassis and Greta Garbo. Baldwin cultivated a decades-long friendship with Jackie Kennedy, who, days after President John F. Kennedy's assassination, moved (with Baldwin's help) out of the White House and into a small house in Georgetown. Years later, Baldwin also designed her home on the island of Scorpios in Greece.

But certainly the most enigmatic of all of Baldwin's projects was the design of reclusive screen actress Greta Garbo's Upper East Side apartment in Manhattan. Only the rarest of individuals were granted the opportunity to step inside this apartment that Baldwin designed.

Throughout his career, Baldwin made a concerted effort to pass on his design knowledge to a new generation of young designers. Like Garrett, Symington, and Wood before him, Baldwin took young decorators with talent and the elusive "it" factor under his wing to mentor them in his vocabulary of "new" design.

Billy Baldwin had a truly successful career. Although he never went to interior design school, he had all the tools and connections necessary to make a success of his chosen life. Neophyte designers should look to him as a role model and take note of his many accomplishments. Baldwin penned a number of design books about his career (most notably, *Billy Baldwin Decorates*) that are essential reading for any designer coming into the business.

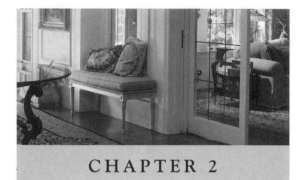

CHAPTER 2

THE STATE OF INTERIOR DESIGN

*Staking Your Claim in a
Boom Industry*

"This work has to do with people and beauty and the timeless activities of domestic life."

—MARK HAMPTON

Now that we have touched on some of the personalities, trends, and organizations that helped transform the interior design industry from a well-heeled hobby into a booming twenty-first-century profession, let's discuss some of the factors presently shaping the climate in the design industry.

STATE OF THE INDUSTRY

Forever changing and eternally the same, interior design has for many years been in a state of flux. Many of the changes have been good for the industry and beneficial for some designers. All in all, however, today's interior design business is unpredictable and requires you to be ready for the unexpected. It truly is amazing to witness how interior design, in all its new forms, continues to grow and evolve at such an astounding clip. Of course, the growth of the industry has had some help (see "The Media's Influence on Design" later in this chapter).

One would imagine, with more than one hundred years of experience under our modern designer belts, that our interest in what we do would have been curtailed over the years. Thankfully, to date, this has proven not to be the case.

Certainly, interior design has taken some bad public relations hits over the years (see "Bad Buzz" later in this chapter), but all things considered, there appears to be no limit to the design industry's reach into the minds (and, more importantly, the wallets) of modern consumers. Some may

15

call today's climate a "design phenomenon," and whatever one chooses to label the present, we hope it lasts another few centuries.

That's a (somewhat) realistic possibility when one considers the flourishing designer landscape. Today, there are so many more potential clients and specialty arms of design that barely existed a decade ago; who's to say what will exist in another twenty years? We certainly never thought we'd see the day when design specialization would become almost as influential in the marketplace as the work of pure designers. Well, it's almost happening.

From today's feng shui consultants, color specialists, and kitchen and bath designers to closet designers and makers of environmentally friendly textile lines, there truly is something out there for any designer (or client) with a specific vision and the will to make it a reality. The current specialty trend may be humbling to some "sacred cow" designers who are used to getting all the glory, but we applaud it. We think design specialization will help fight any future creative stagnation and prevent Microsoft-like design monopolies from taking hold of the industry by keeping design "players" fresh, diversified, and on the cutting edge of popular culture and consumer demand.

While some designers (like us) praise the natural segmentation of the industry as a positive step, others believe it is causing a growing divide among the design ranks and the industry as a whole. It's hard to argue that the business of interior design isn't more segmented (or divided) than ever before—because it is. But it's just as hard to argue that the design of interiors (in all its forms) has ever been more popular than it is right now—because it hasn't. So what's wrong with a little free trade? Can't we all just get along? Maybe.

If the world hasn't yet seen modern design's influence on global culture reach its zenith, then heaven knows how far this current wave of interest will take us. For designers of all ages, it truly is an exciting time to be alive.

Interior design in all its current incarnations is still all the rage. Look around. Everyone (and we mean everyone) is doing it. From birds to bees, to educated fleas, and even architects, the world continues to be fascinated with our art. Design has stormed the modern zeitgeist and taken no prisoners. Let us count the ways:

- The design lexicon has entered the world of the mainstream.
- Lifestyle gurus are teaching interior design to millions through the magic of cable television.
- Design magazines line the shelves of every newsstand on earth.

- Design specialists are honing in on particular segments of the industry—from designing kitchens, bathrooms, and rec rooms to closets, corporate cafeterias, and retirement communities.

- Specialty product lines and boutique shops are everywhere.

- Unqualified amateurs have taken to trying their hand at design.

All the while, professional designers, like us, continue to do our work very well.

Why are so many people obsessed with design? Because interior design is a luxury industry, of course! Like fine cuisine, fine design is glamorous, decadent, and so far removed from the lifestyles of 99 percent of the universe that the media coverage may seem to some like a transmission from another more stylish planet.

Like it or not, the cable television dial—especially channels devoted to improving the lifestyles of American consumers—has propelled the once staid design profession into the pantheon of pop culture "cool." That's right, you heard us: We're cool. As for whether we'll be considered cool in twenty years, we think it's probable.

THE DESIGNER AS MODERN TASTEMAKER

All of you wired into "what's happening" may have noticed that in the past ten years, a hybrid form of designer—the interior designer as media personality—has risen to the prominent role of influential global tastemaker. These media designers are lifestyle forces on the pop culture scene, and they have the ability to impact the way consumers desperate for style and taste view themselves, their environs, and their lives. They influence the perceptions of form, function, comfort, and aesthetic beauty—and most importantly, these media designers determine what is considered cool. Do you see interior design dropping off their top-ten lists anytime soon?

Considering the era in which we live, all designers should thank their lucky stars for the subjectivity of taste. If taste were objective, most designers would be out of a job, wouldn't we? So many people in this world believe they have "good taste" while really not seeming like they have a clue. But like DNA, every human has a different set of likes and dislikes when it comes to design. So who says what good taste is and is not? If a client hires you to design their space, you do.

This brings us to an unspoken variable in the current "designer phenomenon," which is that most Americans will continue to need the help of professional designers. To this day, even the most revered designers are often left scratching their heads, wondering why their clients gravitate to certain things. Most of the time, there are no hard answers, because taste is a moving target.

Why is there such a shroud of mystery to the art of design? Taste is subjective. There is no universal answer. There are a million different answers and a million and one effective ways of doing a project. But which is the perfect answer for your potentially cranky client? Who knows? It's a mystery—now go solve it! Style will always be a moving target. You'll find each design project you undertake in your career to be a unique mystery that you and your client must solve together. What works for one client may not work for another. Who knows why? All we know is that the variability is what makes our profession so much fun.

For some, "good taste" is a God-given gift, while for others, to some extent, it can be learned. Like all other aspects of the job (business development, marketing, sourcing, client relations, office management, etc.), designers must continue to sharpen their aesthetic skills through education and gained experience in order to improve their ability to see the world around them clearly.

Remember, good taste isn't so much about cost; it's about style and execution. Designers must be on point when analyzing the lines, execution, and finish of a design to ascertain what's in good taste and what is just trash.

THE MODERN DESIGNER'S CHALLENGE

Now that we've traced the ascent, evolution, and near saturation of our collective consciousness by modern design, let's talk about what's waiting for young designers when they join the "real world." As we said in chapter 1, to prosper in the business of interior design, they must not only be talented, but also develop agile business minds to go with their creative designer souls.

While it's true that there is a much larger market for interior designers than ever before, gone are the days when you can just open an office, hang a shingle, and expect people to walk through the door. Out of the glut of professionals and amateurs on the scene today, only the best make a lifetime career of the business. Like in most industries, only the strong survive, while purveyors of fraudulence die a quick death or go to work in sales.

These stories are meant to scare you, but don't let them. You are no fake; you can do it all, right? That's a good thing, because designers entering the "fray of today" will soon be asked to do everything under the sun for their clients. It is the nature of the modern game: Interior designers rarely just design blueprints or shell out advice anymore—they run a complete show.

Much like architects, as designers, we make client dreams come true by envisioning a masterpiece and then overseeing its construction through the management of a myriad of micro-projects that lead to the ultimate goal. That means designers must not only be proficient in the art of design, but also in its organization, project management, client relations, ordering, billing, and so forth.

So Many Functions, So Little Time

Whether you'll be capable of meeting all of your future job's business requirements remains to be seen, but know that while most aspiring designers fail miserably, many (in time) prove successful by becoming career jacks-of-all-trades. Their wide-ranging skill sets may include any or all of the following designer roles:

- Design maestro
- Client liaison
- Project manager
- Color and spatial visionary
- Conceptual artist
- Project planner
- Marketing executive
- Public relations guru
- Office manager
- Business developer
- Product designer
- Motivator

Sounds daunting, doesn't it? But that's life in today's landscape, where interior designers must compete in a complex business that's often misunderstood by their clients, their spouse, their children, and the mainstream public. The fact that being a modern interior designer is at least two full-time jobs (artist and businessperson) explains why so many talented designers with outstanding taste and design skills still crash and burn. They simply can't muster the business sense to make it.

Here's a tip: Don't follow in the footsteps of so many dilettantes fresh out of school who made the mistake of spending too much time on aesthetics and forgot the business aspect of the game. Most of these naïve souls were simply shocked to find out that business determines such a large part of one's success. Perhaps they couldn't face the hard reality that, yes, designers are artists, but art and good intentions alone will get you nowhere in this world. The fact of the matter is that, though the love of color, pattern, space, and design schemes is what convinced some of you to drop eighty grand on a design education, it will not keep you in the business unless you have what it takes to make a living doing what you love. Projects must be tackled with a business mentality, and viewed holistically while understanding the purpose of all the variables that make a great design vision into an extraordinary reality.

Competition Is Fierce

While we all appreciate the raving popularity of what we do for a living, understand that our profession's aforementioned overall health may, in fact, be hazardous to the health of your burgeoning career. According to the professional interior design network Designing Profits, Inc. (more on them later), there are approximately forty thousand individuals in America currently practicing as professional interior designers. That figure does not include the thousands of design students (like you) who are about to join the race. Let that sink in for a moment.

We feel there's enough business to go around, especially for professional designers with talent and an acute business sense. Yet, not only do modern designers compete against each other in today's landscape; we also compete against do-it-yourself (DIY) design shows that have mass impregnated the minds of millions of potential clients.

These shows are a designer's enemy. Their aim is to take away your business by convincing people with DIY fever that they, too, could design their space if only they had a little direction and the tools. Some swear by the messages of empowerment, while others—mostly frustrated, out-of-work designers—just swear. We suggest that you keep the end product in mind. Hiring a professional designer will almost always bring better results for clients than if they do it themselves.

UNDERSTANDING THE MODERN CLIENT

Because of the duties, challenges, and pitfalls a young designer will likely encounter coming out of design school, understanding the needs of the modern client is probably the most essential element for designers entering the modern design landscape.

One caveat for the next few pages: We're going to be firing off copious generalities, numerous sweeping statements, and loads of extrapolations. So, take our client stereotyping with a grain of salt, then get out there and create your own individual definition for the modern client. As we've said, every client is different.

Some of you greenhorns may be surprised to learn that many of today's modern clients don't live in multimillion-dollar mansions. Young designers will find that modern clients are young professionals with good jobs and disposable incomes who live in flats, condominiums, apartments, or lofts.

Though they pay close attention to their living environments, most modern clients do not have the time, inclination, or skills to design a living space to their liking. They need help. So, what do they do? Barring an outbreak of DIY fever, they hire an interior designer.

Typical modern clients may not be millionaires, but they appreciate what fine design can do for them and their ever-improving lifestyles. While the vast majority of modern clients aren't interested in living in Hearst Castle, they are interested in designing a personal living space that isn't so much about the quantity as the quality of life. So, how do modern clients choose which designer to hire? Although everyone has different motives, most clients hire designers who can deliver a stylish, functional space. Others hire designers because of name, reputation, or the style or genre in which the designer works.

Function, Comfort, and Space

Typically, the modern client's budget will be fairly strict on most projects and will meet their needs without being out of this world. Their preferred design is less about glamour and more about comfort, space maximization, and, if designing a commercial space, creating a "profitable" environment.

Function, in particular, has become one of the most important aspects of design for both residential and commercial interiors. After all, everyone wants to make the most of what they have, so designers, in turn, are asked to create efficient designs that maximize space. Comfort and space are also of particular importance, especially to the many modern clients who live and work in urban centers. Because space is at such a premium in an urban setting, interior designers help clients cope with the challenges inherent in living in a large city.

Don't discount the impact these three facets of design (function, comfort, and space) will have on your design career. They continue to impact and change the way the industry deals with clients. We no longer see the work of iconic designers like Billie Haines, who created lavish interiors for movie star clientele, as relevant to our business. As opulent as today's designs can be, they must first and foremost meet the demanding criteria of contemporary clients.

The Modern Elite Client

We won't spend much time discussing elite clients, as they haven't changed a bit since the design industry took shape. We should know; we've been practicing luxury residential interior design for a combined fifty-four years. Elite clients often hire designers to remodel one of their multiple homes and tend to work with interior designers who have a name brand, as most of these elite clients do. Unless you are related to someone famous, it is difficult to land a job with a modern elite client. They are less interested in hiring young talent than in hiring an elite designer.

This means the majority of you will almost certainly be working (at least at the outset of your career) with the typical modern client described earlier. And believe us, that's okay. We worked with young professionals too when we were starting out, and we still work with them from time to time. Why? Because they are a young designer's bread and butter. They are your people, so go to them.

That said, understanding the reality of the business doesn't mean one should think small. If you have ambitious dreams of landing a big kahuna right out of the gate, the trick is to think big, act big, and carry a good-looking design stick. (It also won't hurt to keep reading until you get to chapter 8, "How to Attract Clients.")

THE GLAMOUR COMPLEX

It's not uncommon to see young designers thinking big, as most students learn about the glamorous part of the design industry long before they know what design is really about. Where do young designers get the misconception that the practice of interior design is one big sensational event?

The media certainly is a convenient scapegoat, but it's not the whole story. Our history plays a huge role. Forty years ago, only a small percentage of the population, the wealthy elite, was hiring designers. Design was not "within reach" for most people. That meant designers (in turn) had to look the part because they were working with wealthy clients. There was a certain decorum to the whole affair, hence the glamorous image.

But things have drastically changed since the halcyon days of the past. Today, any person can hire a designer; there's even a mega-chain called Design Within Reach, where "normal" people decorate their living spaces with designer furniture, products, and accessories. Yet, designers continue to feed the alluring image. Perhaps this is because many designers prefer to view life through rose-colored glasses and think of themselves as glamour icons. We've certainly met a few of them in our day. We're not here to slam them—what they do is fine if they drop the act long enough to see through the looking glass and into the face of reality. Why is "being real" so important? It's because in this industry, there are so many who aren't.

Believe us: Failing to keep your feet on the ground can result in tragedy right out of the gate. Even if you become an overnight success and suddenly find yourself hobnobbing with elite clientele, as a young designer, you must know from the get-go that glamour is only 10 percent of the business. If you confuse the importance of living lavishly with the importance of paying your bills on time, you are going to be dead in the water. Shall we break down the difference between "the glamour" and "the business"? For the record, here it goes:

The Glamour of Design

- Meeting glamorous clients
- Traveling to exotic locations
- Dressing sharply
- Shopping with clients
- Lunching with clients
- Going over design projects in opulent environs
- Visiting showrooms
- Attending glamorous social events
- Going to events that cater to designers
- Having work published in design magazines
- Being featured on design shows
- Becoming a designer (media) personality

The Business of Design

- Having a clear thought process
- Having clarity of vision
- Selling your concepts
- Organizing and executing the plan
- Managing a team of business allies
- Selling art, furniture, and accessories
- Writing purchase orders and invoices
- Overseeing installations and the delivery of goods
- Getting vendors to accommodate your clients' needs
- Dealing with problem issues that arise

- Communicating your vision
- Paying your bills on time
- Following through relentlessly
- Acquiring new clients and client relations

Now that you understand how image and reality can collide in the world of interior design, keep in mind the difference between glamour and the business and don't let anyone wearing rose-colored glasses tell you otherwise.

All the abounding misconceptions about "what interior designers really do" can be traced back to a lack of real-world education from design schools, design mentors, and our professional organizations. One excellent remedy for all of our misconceptions would be to establish some kind of formal apprenticeship program for young, fresh-out-of-school designers who need to know what being a professional is really all about. Sounds like a pretty good idea, doesn't it? Then why hasn't someone implemented it?

The problem is that no one (to date) has had the authority to lay down a mandate. However, three groups appear capable of taking ownership and offering continued real-world education for postgraduates:

- Design schools
- Professional design organizations
- State legislatures

Until someone steps up, it's ultimately up to existing professional interior designers to bestow professional experience and real-world education on our less experienced brethren. That's one reason why we decided to write this book.

Mentors are in greater demand than ever before, and in the interior design world of today, it sometimes feels as if the inmates are running the asylum. Some readers may be appalled to learn that in many parts of the United States, a person with no experience, license, degree, or paperwork can print up business cards, open up shop, and claim to be an interior designer. These "paper" designers may not be formally trained by a design school or have apprenticed anywhere on earth, and they may not know damask from toile or be professionally certified. And yet, in many states (California, for example), anyone with the necessary resources can legally claim the design profession as their own. This may be sickening, but it is also not surprising.

Again, just look at our history. A hundred years ago, one could argue that every interior decorator in business was a pretender. Why? The profession didn't technically exist.

In our minds, some of today's "paper" designers are scions of the original decorator archetype: the ambitious "ladies with taste" who were neither classically trained nor experienced but had the willpower and the means to become designers. What is the biggest difference between the two? Probably the fact that the socialite designers of yesteryear could get away with inconsistent business tactics. There was no one who was going to stop them.

The "ladies with taste" were rich and affable, socially connected, and not entirely color-blind, and the rest of the world was completely unfamiliar with their art as a business. Their clients did not dare question their unconventional behavior, but rather expected these socialite designers to be mysterious magic makers.

How do you think some of the less-talented pioneering ladies would fare in the twenty-first century? With all the competition, public attention, and media scrutiny, we imagine that many of them would have to be extremely rich and well-connected to succeed in today's world of design.

Speculations aside, we know of a few modern-day "paper" decorette designers in Carmel, California, who aren't necessarily revered like their predecessors but are nevertheless making a go of it by tapping into that same magic from years gone by: wads of money, loads of connections, fair to middling talent, and, frankly, not much else.

Highlighting the connection between the socialite designers of the past and the "paper" decorette designers of today doesn't tell the entire story. Here are some practical reasons why there continues to be a proliferation of "paper" designers in the industry:

- Industry regulations in many states are extremely lax.
- Most clients still don't fully understand what a designer does.
- "Paper" designers can quickly set up shop and appear to be professionals.
- Smooth-talking pretenders can get a foot in the industry door by selling their "act" to only a few individual home owners.
- Many outside the industry think being a designer is easy.

Most of today's "paper" decorette designers think the job of designing is easy; they aren't looking at it as a profession. This is because most unqualified individuals trying to jump into the design game do so for all the wrong reasons: money, prestige, exposure to the rich and famous, and lifestyle. They seem to have a hard time understanding that interior design is a business; it's not just running around and having lunch with glamorous friends.

BAD BUZZ

In case you didn't get the memo, interior design is a calling that comes with some baggage. Some of these impediments are fairly modern (see "The Pricing War" in chapter 6), while other pieces, like our stereotypical "flakey diva" reputation, are as old as the profession itself. This metaphorical baggage pile up means that designers today (especially young, inexperienced designers) face an uphill battle in carving out a successful career. Every designer entering the marketplace must overcome the profession's long-standing reputation for being unorganized, inconsistent, and, yes, flakey.

What has hurt public perception the most over the years has been shoddy individuals doing a disservice to the profession by calling themselves interior designers. Add the industry's long-running feud over price and designer fee structures (see chapter 6) to the mix, and one can see how all the inconsistent behavior has damaged our credibility with important allies like prospective clients, repeat clients, and the media.

While some in the design community believe our "perception issues" will naturally work out over time, that may not be the case. Thanks to the media and the digital age, the entire globe has been able to monitor closely the behavior of far too many charlatans in our designer henhouse. We call it "bad buzz," and our industry has gotten its share over the past one hundred years. But where does bad buzz come from?

The answer is anywhere and everywhere. Some clients hear bad buzz from a hyperbolic country club matron who "just had the worst experience" of her life "working with so-and-so designer," while others learn about it through design-related stories in the media. Before the age of the Internet, bad word of mouth traveled ten times faster than good news. So, how quickly do you think bad word of mouth travels now? It's close to the speed of light.

Media influence aside, some of the most persistent circulators of bad buzz are "queen bee" repeat clients who simply never get over a frustrating experience they had working with a dizzying cast of unprofessional designers. Befuddled by the wildly fluctuating industry standards, how do you imagine most of these unsatisfied, often affluent queen bee clients show their displeasure? You got it: by complaining to any drone who will listen.

A Bad First Experience

Bad publicity and bad word of mouth aren't the only kinds of negative buzz that send today's reputable designers into a damage-control frenzy. There is an even more potent, more common strain of bad buzz that tends to have a permanent souring effect on prospective clients: first-hand experience.

Let's say we have a "virgin" client who doesn't watch the design shows, hasn't picked up a design rag, and avoids all gossip at the country club. She is interested in having her home redesigned, but isn't sure what kind of designer she should hire. So, after two initial phone calls, she arranges an in-home consultation with two possible designers, who we'll call Designer One and Designer Two. Both candidates were referred by trustworthy friends and are ASID-certified professionals with degrees from reputable design schools.

Designer One arrives for the consultation and says:

> I am very interested in your project but can't tell you exactly how long it will take to complete. I also cannot give you an exact budget, but will be happy to work with you on a cost-plus basis for the procurement of every piece of furniture, fabric, and accessories.
>
> In addition, I require a small deposit of 30 percent of the cost to place orders. The balance will be due once I have all the freight bills and additional charges ready for invoicing. I know most designers charge fees for their time, but in order to sweeten the deal and secure the project, I'm not going to charge for my design time.

"Wow," the client says. "Even though I have no idea of Designer One's vision or timetable, or how much money I'm going to spend, it sounds almost too good to be true. But let's hold off on any decisions until after the next consultation."

Next up is Designer Two, who says:

> After listening to your needs, I can tell you with all confidence your project will take six months to complete and will cost a total of X amount.
>
> However, as an established professional with an office and a staff to keep, my design fee, payable in advance, is Y and my hourly fee is Z. In addition, all items procured through my office will be billed at a presented price [see chapter 6, Defining Your Dream] and will require a deposit of sixty percent of that price to place the order. The balance will be due before delivery."

If both of the designers' portfolios look good and both have good reputations as professionals, the trendy choice would be to choose Designer

One. With this selection, the client could see all the money that is being spent and passive-aggressively control the project herself.

Of course, if Designer One routinely gives this kind of deal to all his clients, what does that say about his skill level and place in the industry? Perhaps Designer One isn't as experienced or talented as Designer Two, who swaggered in with an exact timeline, precise numbers, and a confident, take-it-or-leave-it approach to the bidding process. Doesn't the more precise bid from Designer Two translate to better quality and service? And if a client wants the best, shouldn't she hire the best?

Dealing with the Bad Buzz

Indoctrinated by the confusion and fear of a first-time experience like the one just mentioned, clients often throw up their arms at the different presentation styles and confusing price differential. They may, with a little help from Martha Stewart, eventually decide to do the redesign themselves. Need we remind our readers that a nation of do-it-yourselfers is not what the design industry wants or needs?

Consequently, until there is some kind of overall uniformity to our business that's mandated from "up on high" by the government or professional organizations, many young designers will be "deemed guilty" until they prove themselves to be trustworthy professionals.

Just like your grandchildren will pay a price for all of the environmental pollution that has occurred over the past one hundred years, many young designers will pay for the bad buzz that originated with the "paper" designers who came before them. This may translate to a young designer having to:

- Spend more time defending pricing methods and business philosophy to clients and prospective clients

- Explain to potential clients what a "professional" designer does and does not do

- Convince existing clients to continue using professional design services after they hear or read yet another "designer horror story" from a friend or in one of the many design magazines

Bad buzz tends to work in cycles and, thanks to the digital media, will never truly go away. Every one of you must learn to deal with the industry's flakey past or fold up your tent and go home.

THE MEDIA'S INFLUENCE ON DESIGN

As we near the finish line in our examination of the design industry's state, we've come to a point where we can finally ask readers, "Who inspired you to try your hand at interior design?" Was it a stylish mother, a savvy teacher, or the work of an architect like Frank Lloyd Wright?

We hasten to guess that it wasn't so much a single person or place as it was a *thing* that inspired you—something that is, to this day, as influential and far-reaching as virtually any other entity on earth. Of course, we're talking about the all-encompassing, world-devouring American media.

Some loathe it, while others adore it, but for most of us, the media's holy trinity (print, television, and film) helped to kindle the first spark of interest in design during our impressionable years. Whether it was the design of *The Brady Bunch* house or that special episode of *Martha Stewart Living*, MTV's *Cribs*, or *Lifestyles of the Rich and Famous*, for most of us, it was the mass media that introduced us to the art and glamour of interior design.

Martha Raised the Bar

The lifestyle phenomenon of today can be traced back to Martha Stewart. The debut of her television show in the early 1990s raised the bar for designers everywhere by inventing the universe of the lifestyle guru who (like many do-it-yourselfers) also just so happened to dabble in interior design. Although she's not a real interior designer (or our cup of tea, for that matter), Martha has done a good job of permanently branding the design craze on the brows of the American public. She has shown the world that there is substantial consumer interest in the packaging of interior design and lifestyle programming.

Design and lifestyle shows have done a great service to our industry by showing the world that you can live with style whether or not you have a ton of money. Thanks to the American media, consumers have become more style conscious, brand conscious, and aware of design as a vocation or as an avocation. This can only be a good thing for designers.

Especially in the last ten years, design shows have gotten increasingly savvy about what clients want to see. From reality series like *Designers' Challenge*, to the do-it-yourself shows, to the popularity of niche programs like *Antiques Roadshow*, there is now enough specialty design-related programming to fill your TiVo until the end of time. Many disagree with what these shows say about designers (and design), but remember, these shows aren't about the business of interior design; they are about entertainment. Though designers aren't always portrayed as rocket scientists, we truly think these shows offer a service to the design industry by raising global awareness of the field.

If you're one of those purists who would like to see the level of professionalism raised on design shows, then we suggest that you appear on one. How else will the world see real designers in action if honest professionals like you aren't appearing to show them how it's done?

We realize that if we're going to talk the talk, we'd also better walk the walk. Hale-Williams Interiors is proud to report that we accepted our own challenge and appeared on the design show *Designers' Challenge* back in 2005. We even won, thank you very much! Now it's your turn.

Not Better or Worse, Just Different

Since, as we've learned in this chapter, interior design has moved out of the exclusive world of the super wealthy and into the world of the mainstream, some observers believe that now is a better time than ever for designers to prosper. Conversely, others feel that it's more difficult for designers starting out to enter the profession, due to the complexity of the business and the enormous amount of competition.

We say that it's not better and it's not worse; it's just different, with a far larger field than ever before on which to strut your stuff. So get to strutting, my friends, and keep these points in mind:

- There is more competition than ever before.
- There are now more diverse opportunities.
- There is a broader range of clients with more money than previously.
- Clients are more knowledgeable than ever before.
- Clients increasingly know what they want.

Remember, it's survival of the fittest in any free marketplace. Only the strongest, smartest, and most adaptable prosper; so be tough, stand by your convictions, believe in your talent, get smart, and learn how to adapt your game to the signs of the times.

CHAPTER 3

CUTTING YOUR TEETH IN THE REAL WORLD

Do You Have the Chops?

"Young designers should understand a career path in
interior design rarely plays out in a straight line."
—GIOI TRAN OF APPLEGATE TRAN INTERIORS

Any further examination of the industry on a macro level would quickly become a superfluous bore, so let's hone in on the micro details that really matter to you tenderfoots right now, like, for example: How do you get a good job fresh out of design school?

FINDING WHERE YOU BELONG

Don't be intimidated by the horror stories. Our goal is to help every young designer reading this book find that perfect seat at the "professional designers' table." And you will … eventually. However, it may take some time and patience before you find that sweet gig with your name on it. So, relax and take a deep breath while we discuss the employment opportunities most of you will find waiting for you after you've been handed that expensive design diploma.

Not to state the obvious, but right out of school, it's essential to get some real work experience. You may think the transition from design dilettante to professional businessperson is going to be seamless because of your talent, royal pedigree, or industry connections, and maybe you are right. Graduates at the top of their class from one of the major design schools will almost certainly get a good job straight out of school.

But odds are that with no experience, no work history, and a design résumé that could fit on a cocktail napkin, you're probably going to find you're just one of the thousands of talented graduates scrambling to land a handful of entry-level positions.

Remember, sometimes even the best students need to experience a few different venues before settling into a specific area of the industry. While some designers immediately know they excel at color pairing or spatial planning, it may take others years to realize they love one aspect of design better than the rest. This is exactly why these "early years" are all about investigation and exploration.

So, get out there and investigate; explore! Don't just expect the perfect job to fall into your lap. Be prepared for the first leg of your journey to potentially require several stops where you'll learn what to do and what not do from multiple design mentors. This will allow you to run a successful business before you find exactly what you're looking for.

Believe it or not, a diverse work experience in the early part of one's career can do wonders for one's character. Good designers will tell you that it's probably a good idea to "cut your teeth" in an assortment of different design-related roles during your "salad days," as it expands your horizons and helps develop your business acumen. Try anything and everything design-related at first, and don't be afraid to say yes, even when you know you're getting in over your head.

The challenge of diving into unknown areas of design, especially areas in which you don't think you have a passion, is one of the most exciting parts of the business. So embrace it, knowing it's an important part of your development that will aid in your growth as a designer and an individual.

It's hard for a lot of young graduates to realize that the worst jobs are actually the ones you know you can do, while the best are the ones that challenge the very essence of your designer soul. In other words, if you think you've got the "chops" to succeed in this business, do your career a favor and take the most challenging job you're offered. We guarantee you will grow into whatever endeavor you undertake.

If you're like most readers, you're not sure what you're passionate about or what you do best. That's okay, because it's all a part of the discovery process. Understanding early on that you are on a personal quest to find your unique passion for design will eventually bring you to a clear idea of what you—and you alone—do best.

While realizing you're as much on a journey of self-discovery as you are searching for a paycheck, where do you start looking for answers? How about with one of the forty thousand professional designers working in America today? Of course, that sounds good, but the majority of today's modern American design firms are actually just one-person operations that don't hire full-time design assistants straight out of school.

Don't let the numbers discourage you. There are still a lot of jobs out there; you just have to be persistent in your search and let the design world know (in every way, shape, and form) that you have arrived and are in the market for a full-time position. You'll find that in life, opportunity can be found in the most unlikely places.

Job Interviewing 101

For those of you out there who've already lined up a job interview (good for you!), here are a few interview tips to get you started. (For a more in-depth discussion, we suggest you read chapter 8, "How to Attract Clients," to learn how to present yourself to potential employers and clients.)

- Arrive on time with as much knowledge of the company as possible.
- Dress appropriately and sharply and be able to speak the company's language.
- Know what kind of work the company does (and doesn't do).
- Research salaries so you know how they pay employees like yourself.
- Know the company staff; any friendly insider will help your cause.
- Educate yourself on company projects that may interest you.

Remember, it's up to you to convince any potential employer that you're interested in what it has to offer. Be sure to leverage every drop of your vast reserves of knowledge, charm, wit, and personality during the interview to "grease the wheels," so to speak.

Who Wants to Be an Entrepreneur?

Now, you may be one of the cocky individuals out there saying, "Slow down, Hale-Williams…interview? I don't need interview tips! Don't you know I'm going to shake up this tired old industry and become my own boss?"

We applaud your confidence and admire your ambition, but one of the first cold, hard facts post graduates quickly realize is that virtually every young designer coming out of school lacks the resources, experience, connections, or tenacity to immediately start his or her own design business. Coming from experience, let us suggest that this is not such a bad thing. Trying to start a business right out of design school can be a messy endeavor that often leads to young designers adopting unsound business practices and making numerous bad decisions.

Of course, that doesn't mean some of you out there won't do it and do it well (see chapter 5, "Plunging Off the Designer High Dive"), but for many of you reading this book, you will surely go to work for somebody straight out of the gate. While we realize watching and learning can sometimes be a frustrating experience when you're ready to get on with your fabulous career, the time and effort spent will make all the difference later.

And frankly, why not let someone else pay for your rookie mistakes? The flipside of this coin is that you may be able to bask in a little of your seasoned employer's reflected glory. That isn't such a bad trade-off, is it?

Considering a Small Firm

If you're considering applying to one of the many small design firms around the country, which staff anywhere from two to ten employees, here are some general factors you should keep in mind whether the firm specializes in residential work, commercial work, or both.

The Pros of Working for a Small Design Firm

- Direct contact with the principal designer
- Working with all clients (big or small)
- Learning from the principal designer
- Working on all aspects of the business
- Potential for rapid advancement and salary increase
- Direct participation in bonus and incentive dollars

The Cons of Working for a Small Design Firm

- Smaller starting salary
- Smaller offices with fewer perks
- No receptionist or support staff
- Small to no benefits package
- Being thrown into the pool and made to swim
- Watching a business be run by the seat of its pants

Considering a Large Firm

If, in your eyes, the negatives listed above greatly outweigh the positives, you're probably going to find yourself jockeying for one of the coveted positions at one of the large design or architecture firms that staff more than ten employees. Be prepared: The competition to "get in" will be tremendous, while the available positions will likely be limited in scope. But don't let that stop you from going for a job that may be a great entry-level position and career stepping-stone. Here are a few general factors you should keep in mind when you apply to one of the large design or architecture firms:

The Pros of Working for a Large Firm

- Earning a weekly salary
- Having a health and retirement benefits package
- Learning the trade as part of a large, well-oiled machine
- Potential to work on a variety of different jobs
- Various in-house mentors
- Lots of support staff (receptionist, librarian, stock manager, etc.)

The Cons of Working for a Large Firm

- Stuck in the same job with no variety
- Little chance for rapid advancement
- Sparse contact with principal designers
- Little to no contact with major clients
- Small bonus participation

Now that you know something about how big firms and small firms usually treat entry-level employees, if you are offered a good job of any kind that challenges your skills, take it!

It doesn't matter if you prefer to work in a more hands-on environment or would rather work for a high-profile design firm; if you're offered a decent position at any good design firm, go for it even if you have some reservations. Why? We're not always the best judges of our talents. You may be surprised to find that aspects of the job interest you more than you thought they would.

Considering a Retail Environment

If you're one of the many designers who can't seem to find work at either a small or a large design or architecture firm, and you're hell-bent on keeping a toe in the design game, you may be tempted to take one of the many sales jobs available in the design industry.

Although positions like representing a product line, working in a retail space, or managing a design showroom are still technically industry jobs, your design skills almost certainly won't be utilized to their full potential. These positions are sales jobs, and although you may be given an opportunity to dabble in the design of interiors, your primary job will be to move product. Here are some general factors you should consider before accepting a retail position in the design industry:

The Pros of Working in a Retail Environment

- Potential to earn a good salary
- Potential for a benefits and retirement package
- Still being in the design industry
- Getting to interact with designers and clients
- Potentially dabbling in design through interaction with customers

The Cons of Working in a Retail Environment

- Earning a living as a salesperson
- Probably not living your dream
- Having wasted a ton of money on a design degree
- Servicing other designers who are doing what you should be doing
- Having little room for career advancement
- High employee turnover often occurs in these positions

Young designers desperate to pay the rent should be warned that although sales positions may still require a good knowledge of design, the potential to earn a substantial salary at an early age has been known to curb one's burning desire to make a living as an interior designer. In other words, once some people get a taste of the "good life" afforded by money, it robs them of their ambition. In the paragraphs below is an example of how the situation could play out if you or any of your design colleagues take a job in retail.

Let's say a fresh-faced designer with a shiny new degree can't find a design job in the "real world," so she takes a position as a sales representative. And surprise, surprise—she finds out she's pretty darn good at sales. So good, in fact, she starts making a good commission...and then she starts making a great commission.

So one day, the sales rep says, "Wow, I'm making a lot of money as a salesperson. Why should I continue trying to be an interior designer? Young designers who work for someone else don't make much money, and young designers who go into business for themselves don't take home a large income because they're constantly investing all their profits back into their business." The sales rep finally decides, "I'm happy right here, thank you very much." And so, another burning fire of ambition is extinguished by the seductive powers of the almighty dollar.

Don't let us get away with implying that taking a job that includes sales is in any way "selling out." Retail work, if that's your cup of tea, is a perfectly respectable venture. For many professional salespeople out there, it's their life's passion.

But we just happen to be writing a book about *our* passion, which is hopefully yours as well: interior design. Hungry designers should be aware that a big-time sales job right out of the gate is a double-edged sword that has slain the dreams of many a young designer. If you're truly passionate about becoming a bona fide professional, be careful not to allow the lure of financial gain to slay your dream.

GAME-PLANNING FOR SUCCESS

Now you're beginning to see what a slippery slope finding your first job can be. No entry-level position will be perfect, and while you don't want to waste years of your career trying to understand how you fit into the world of design, it's difficult to know where your true passion will lead you. How should neophytes combat these uncertain early days?

Create a Master Plan

Craft a master plan for your career right now. This is your long-range road map, and you are the only one who knows what dreams and challenges it contains. If you haven't written one yet, do it! But what if you aren't sure about anything? It doesn't matter. Make a master plan anyway. It's not going to be perfect, so who cares? No plan is perfect; just put it on paper and watch how it and you evolve together. Remember, if you don't know what you want to do, how in the world do you expect to get there? Rarely does fate answer a silent bell.

Be Realistic

Even for the most ambitious designers, it helps if you write some reality into your master blueprint. For example, come to the understanding that you probably aren't going to find a job right off the bat where you gain comprehensive design experience while doing it all. That's why they call them entry-level positions; most consist of tasks better left to a design apprentice.

Plan for the fact that in the early part of your career, you'll have to accept jobs you wouldn't normally take in order to get to where you want to be. Your planning just may result in your having the clarity of mind to seize an employment opportunity not for the positional duties, but because the firm offering it has a great reputation or the job will give you access to industry connections. Now you are thinking of your future. Feels good, doesn't it?

Have a Timeline for Everything

When you're finally offered a job, it's essential that you understand how it fits into your master plan before you agree to the terms. Once you clearly see how a potential job can be a stepping-stone to something greater, sign the contract; then, build a timeline into your master plan. Your timeline contains the specific and, usually, short-term goals, as opposed to your master plan, which is the overview of your career.

Some timelines may be as simple as saying, "I'm going to give this job six months before I reevaluate; then, if I'm not happy with my progress, I'll move on to the next step," while others may be more complex deliberations where you establish a timeline for a potential career at a particular firm. Regardless of scope, get in the habit of building timelines for every professional endeavor you undertake and include them in your master plan.

Once you agree on a timeline, the most important part is sticking to it. Never let external factors like the daily grind, office politics, or personal emotions get in the way of your goals. This is business, remember?

Foster the Right Attitude

Speaking of "the daily grind," once you're finally on the job, whether it is with a small or large firm, go in with the mindset that you're there to learn. Even if you graduated at the top of your class and know you're destined to become the most influential designer of the twenty-first century, don't get ahead of yourself. You just may find that you have more to learn about the business than you think.

Set the tone early. Go into your first day like the walking, talking embodiment of a tabula rasa (clean slate)—you're there to absorb fully every lesson that comes your way. If they ask you to do AutoCAD in the corner all day, then do AutoCAD to the best of your abilities! Consider whatever menial tasks you're given as an opportunity to "show your stuff" while perfecting one of your many design-related skills. After all, interior design is such a complex business; this may be the only chance in your career to focus on something as specific as perfecting your AutoCAD skills for weeks on end while getting paid to do so.

Your start is all about how you view it. If you're certain you're mired in the gallows with no hope for the future, then that is exactly where you will be. Take it from us: Most of the successful endeavors you undertake in your life can be traced back to your attitude going into the venture.

Remember the wise man who said, "Happiness is a state of mind." At this point in your budding career, you might find yourself plodding away at some entry-level position while wondering, Is this all there is? The answer to your question is a resounding No. There is so much more out there for individuals who are patient and know how to make things happen. The question is, Are you one of those people?

While you consider whether you are the type of person who "lets things happen" or "makes things happen," know that the growing pains you're feeling are quite common. They are so common, in fact, that they've become a long-standing tradition in our industry. We call these growing pains "paying your dues."

Never heard of paying your dues? You must be either as good as you say or as naïve as we think. The truth is, we all had to start at the bottom of the food chain; you will, too, so get used to the idea. It could be worse. Many design graduates never work a single day in the design business.

We aren't going to get into why something like this occurs—one could write a series of books on the subject—but believe us: It happens all the time. So be thankful you have a design degree, a good first job, a realistic master plan already in progress, and a specific timeline for the steps you must take to get you where you need to be. Stop complaining and get to work.

CASE STUDY: APPLEGATE TRAN INTERIORS

Now that you've digested some of our pearls of wisdom on the opportunities and pitfalls that await you in today's entry-level employment landscape, we'd like to hand the microphone over to a colleague whose perspective (we believe) is a perfect complement to our curriculum.

Gioi Tran, of Applegate Tran Interiors, is an internationally recognized designer and an excellent teacher of interior design at the University of California at Berkeley as well as the San Francisco Art Academy. With more than fifteen years of experience in residential and commercial design, we think he's an apt selection for our case study. He relates his experience below.

Applegate Tran Interiors

Over the years, I've had the opportunity to interact with a lot of different design students and up-and-coming designers who all think they know everything about the industry before they have earned a nickel as a professional. What do I tell my callow pupils? Dream on! You may think you know it all, but really, you haven't got a clue.

I know this because I knew nothing when I got out of design school. Sure, I had a smart portfolio and knew I had talent, but that was about it. Yet, I too was full of hubris, so certain I was ready to go to war when I wasn't. I suppose it's all part of the "designer makeup" to be brimming with confidence; but learn to curb that urge, young designers—especially at the beginning of your career. You need to learn a few things before you start upstaging your elders.

So many young people these days don't fully understand what being a professional designer is all about. Perhaps it's the fault of the design schools, or just the intrinsic nature of the industry (where the competition is stiff and mentors are few and far between), but I find myself bestowing the same lessons (again and again) to different students.

It's a Business!

One of my biggest lessons is the same one Robert and Tom have been beating into you for the past few chapters: Get out there and learn the skills you need to succeed beyond the creative aspects! Being creative is fabulous and essential, but it will only get you so far. The rest of the business, which largely goes untaught in most design schools, is where you will make or break your career. Believe it.

As Robert and Tom say, most students don't "get" that, to succeed in design, one must master business skills like marketing, follow-through, and organization (to name a few). And I'm just talking about the skills that are essential for being a successful interior designer—not those that are necessary for running a successful design firm, which we'll get to later.

Interior design has always been an extremely hard business to break into because there are no guidelines, few set rules, and a lack of overall structure to the way most of us do business. But that doesn't mean business fundamentals don't apply—they do! You had better have your ducks in a row if you are entering today's marketplace, because this is a big-time, free-trade industry that's more difficult to crack than ever before, due to the growing popularity of design around the world. Competition is everywhere! The global floodgates are wide open, which means anyone who wants to can get in.

Don't ever think that the design diploma you're holding is somehow going to be your key to the kingdom. Today, it's less about what they teach you in school and more about what you do with the real-world skills you learn "on the fly" working in the private sector.

More and more, the "new players" in the industry are rising to the top, not because of their elite educations but because of their superior tenacity, innovative business models, and ability to execute like no other. Throw in an array of finely tuned business methods, a great master plan, and some solid financial backing, and you've got a recipe for success. Who cares about a formal education anymore? No one, really.

One huge factor in the current popularity of interior design is that everyone thinks they can do it. Why? Because it's technically true! Anyone in the world can walk in off the street tomorrow, launch a furniture line, and open a showroom without having any formal knowledge of or reputation in the industry.

Not everyone can be ASID-certified, but anyone can call him- or herself a decorator in the United States: anyone. This blurs the line between "professional" and "amateur" but, as I see it, that's not such a bad thing. Today's swinging-door policy is really just Darwinism or natural selection at its finest. And who can disagree with the survival of the fittest? I say, Let the best designers win.

Getting Out There

If you're like me, you won't begin to truly realize your strong points until you start working. When I graduated, I knew I wanted to do residential design. I had a vision of what it would be like, but I really had to "get out there" to understand who I really was and what I wanted to do with my career. Then, one day, while doing the day-to-day stuff, I finally realized what drove me to become a designer. It will happen to you, too.

As a young designer, it's best to try everything as long as you know where you want to be. You can even go to work for an architecture firm and focus on specific aspects of the business (like renderings or building models) if that's something that interests you. There's so much diversity to choose from—especially if you are living in a big market city. My advice to you is to understand from day one what you want from your career, and let that knowledge guide you to where you need to be.

As a practice, it's hard for young designers to survive all the mishaps that are going to happen, especially when you start your own business. That's why it's a good idea to spend some time working for a design firm right out of design school. It will give you real-world experience and will usually provide the wake-up call you need.

And who knows? Once you find out what you do well, maybe you'll realize you shouldn't have your own business at all. Perhaps you'll find it's best for you to work for somebody else and specialize in a specific area of the business, like space design, color, materials, lighting, etc. Everyone is different.

That's why when students ask me how they should go about doing certain things, I say, "I can tell you how I do things today, and I can tell you how I did things ten years ago. But what you have to do is take from my experience and find out how you will do it." Sounds like a lot of double-talk, doesn't it? But it's true. I honestly can't tell you what will work best for you. Only you can find that out for yourself.

Going Into Business for Yourself

Some of my more ambitious students decide to go into business for themselves, and the first question they ask is, "How do I avoid the problem client?" I reply that starting out, young designers can't pick and choose. Firms like Hale-Williams and Applegate Tran can avoid working with problem clients by seeing them coming from a mile away and saying No, because we can afford it.

As for young designers starting a business, they unfortunately do not have the same luxury. Young designers need clients to get established in the business. Consequently, barring the occasional absolutely horrible client, they have to do the best they can to satisfy any client they can get.

Problem Clients

Beware, young entrepreneurs; "difficult" clients are typically the ones who will gravitate to you. Here's why:

- They want a bargain.

- They want to control the project.

- They only want specific tasks completed, and at the right price.

Difficult clients usually avoid firms like Applegate Tran or Hale-Williams because they see our names and all the publications in which we've been featured, and they realize that we are real design firms and assume that we're probably too expensive for them. So, what do we do? We refer them to a young designer who needs the business. That's reality.

Here's another modern reality: Clients do not understand what it takes to be an interior designer; they never have. Rarely will you meet a client who is educated about how a professional designer does business. One would think, with all the design shows on television, that some people would learn how we do business by osmosis. But that's never the case.

The common result of this modern complex is that a clueless client, after being paired with an inexperienced designer, turns into a difficult client. This is usually not because they are intentionally controlling or evil but because they don't know how the process works. So, naturally, they get scared.

Here is how trouble usually starts brewing: A clueless client hires a designer who puts together a project plan that the client can't visualize. This leads to clients questioning rates and charges because they can't understand the value in buying something intangible that won't come together for six or nine months.

While these clients are having trouble visualizing the finished product, guess what? They continue to receive invoices and hourly bills, which make them either freak out or refuse to approve the project because they don't trust the designer.

This type of scenario happens all the time, especially to young design entrepreneurs. Why? Because most clients don't trust their own judgment, so how in the world can they trust some "kid designer" who has no reputation or experience?

Things They Don't Teach You in Design School

Here's another real-world scenario you won't find in a design book. Let's say you're a designer who charges by the hour and you are working on a design concept for a residential space. There may be times when you sit for hours, *designing in your head; and while it may only take you half an hour to draw it all up on paper, all the concepts and ideas were percolating upstairs for hours. How should you, as a designer, bill for your time?*

This is a tough question, even for me. It is hard for a client to justify paying for a "designer brainstorm." But quandaries such as this are the unique challenges a designer must face every day. You can't "not charge" the client and expect to stay in business; so what should you do?

Designers must sell clients not only on their talent and vision, but also on their creative process. All designers have a method to their madness, but unless you're a savvy salesperson and an excellent communicator, your clients will just see the madness and miss the method. It's up to you to show them the way.

Did you learn that in design school? I didn't think so! Young designers should be prepared for these kinds of real-world challenges—like billing quandaries and educating uneasy clients concerning the way you do business. It's all a part of the game, and no one ever fully understands the game until they actually get out there and play it.

Linear Career Paths Are Old School

Although I tell students with a clear vision of their career path to keep moving forward in the same direction, you never know when a new opportunity will take you on a little diversion. For some, this diversion may be just that—a dead-end side alley. But for others, a diversion may become a totally different type of design career that turns out to be much better than the original plan.

Here's a little joke I tell my students: "How do you make God laugh? You make a plan." Life is about improvisation and being open to new opportunities, so it's good to embrace possibility while you're young. Know that you're never going to get where you want to be via a straight path. Life doesn't work that way. Opportunity will come along when you least expect it, so be prepared.

If you take away one lesson from me, let it be this: Find a way to ignite your internal tenacity and fearlessness to "just do it," whatever "it" is for you. Yes, you're going to fail, but you'll try again, and you'll do better the next time. Incremental success leads to great success in this life. I suggest that you work on building your internal fire so that you can be successful no matter what you do. And don't worry about what you don't know or think you do know. On the next project, you'll find yourself saying, Well, I just learned something new.

THE BOTTOM LINE ON DIVING IN

We've said it before and we'll say it again: In the twenty-first-century marketplace, there is an enormous interest in our profession. This means that, in a country where there are twenty-four-hour television channels dedicated to interior design and everyone has seemingly piled onto the designer bandwagon, there are loads of opportunities out there for young designers to break into the business. Just don't necessarily expect to know what your opportunity will look like until you see it.

If you can come to grips with the fact that no designer coming out of design school is immediately going to earn $100,000 per year, have the best clients, garner the best press, drive the best automobile, live in the best apartment, wear the best clothes, or work for the best business in town, then you may be able to take full advantage of this stage of your career.

It's what we call the "continued education phase" of your career, in which you have a wonderful opportunity to get in the door somewhere, learn the business of interior design from the ground up, and apply that knowledge to being the very best designer you can be. If this sounds exciting, that's because it is. You will be living your passion, and not many people can say that. Now get to work.

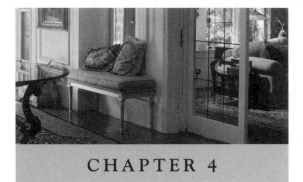

UNDERSTANDING DESIGN SEGMENTS

The Art of Interior Design

> "I have a lot of love to give, but I don't know
> where to put it."
> —WILLIAM H. MACY, FROM THE MOVIE *MAGNOLIA*
> (1999)

If you've gotten this far in your design education, you know that the primary function of an interior designer is to plan and execute the design of interior spaces. But what kind of spaces are for you? Young designers should begin to weigh this fundamental question during the early part of their training and career.

Most designers will agree that there are five major interior design fields: residential design, nonresidential or commercial design, product design, retail design (designing within a retail environment), and architectural design. Although design specialization is not mandatory (there are many designers who find it rewarding to do it all), having a good idea about which way you lean will help you better understand your business, your clients, and your goals. We all have to start somewhere, so don't agonize over the decision. You can always adapt your business down the road.

Many designers and design firms evolve to specialize in different kinds of work during their business lives, but the truth is, most of us tend to find a niche and stick with it. It's human nature and the "American way" to hone your craft in a specialized area. So, which segment should you choose?

RESIDENTIAL DESIGN

As you know, residential interior design is our forte and is intended for private domiciles where individual persons or families live. Boutique hotels, private jets, guest homes, vacation condos, and yachts can be considered

49

residential projects if the owners of these spaces hire a designer to work for them or members of their family.

If a commercial owner hires you to design a space that will be occupied by another person, some designers may consider this non residential work—it really depends on who you ask. The reason we split hairs is because there is a distinct difference in the relationship between the client and the designer when working on residential versus non residential projects. In fact, most designers will tell you that the biggest contrasts in overall investment, clientele, complexity of the project, and business relationships come when comparing residential and non residential projects.

Residential projects are far more personal work. We personally love working in the residential design segment, as we truly believe homes are at the very heart and essence of family. We enjoy the exposure to the luxurious surroundings of our clientele and find this segment of the business to be more glamorous than commercial design. In addition, the selection of goods and products for residential homes far surpasses the selection for commercial projects—so for us, it's a lot more fun.

There is also a lot more money in this type of design and (in our experience) the rewards tend to be more "warm and fuzzy" than in the other segments. Residential design may not be for everyone, but it was a natural fit for us since all of our interior design heroes—like Billy Baldwin, Michael Taylor, Mark Hampton, Rose Cumming, John Saladino, and Juan Pablo Molyneux—were residential designers.

In evaluating whether residential design is for you, remember that entry into the residential marketplace is almost always easier than getting your foot in the commercial design door. Word of mouth tends to work better in the residential field, and not only is the capital investment less, but it's easier to land clients through social settings such as country clubs, PTA meetings, churches, and the like. One can truly create a residential interior design business in a single room of one's home; this is usually not the case with commercial design.

The Psychology of Residential Design

To start a business in the residential world, an interior designer should be able to strike up (and then maintain) a genuine rapport with virtually any "type" of client. We aren't saying that you must learn to tolerate insane clients. It's up to you to judge whether a client is working with all the necessary marbles. What we mean is: Designers and clients must have a good working relationship in order to build a shared vision for a private space. Never underestimate the power of psychology in the creation of residential environments; it is all part of our art.

As residential designers, our job is to interpret dreams as much as reality, so it will behoove you to sharpen your ability to accurately "read" people. This is a huge part of the process. Some clients haven't a clue as to how to communicate what they want, so young designers must have patience and a clear, insightful vision of their own in order to come up with a realistic blueprint that blends form and function within the parameters of a collective vision.

Residential design is all about shaping a mutual vision between the client and the designer of what a space can and should be. This mind-melding process can be tricky. So, when planning, don't spare the details under the false premise that you and your client share an unspoken bond that will carry you through the project. Many have perished under this assumption.

Residential designers must be the walking, talking embodiments of flexible strength. This is because with some projects, you're going to feel like a client has crossed the line by asking you to become the pivotal hub of their household. Regardless of how indispensable they make you feel, it's unlikely your client is interested in adopting you. We highly suggest you keep the relationship professional at all times.

The Scope of Residential Projects

Residential projects may require you to plan and execute the design of an entire residence or only a portion of a space. Believe it or not, some clients will hire you to design a single room, remodel their closet, or procure a single piece of furniture. Like life, every project is different, so understand that residential projects may include all or some of the following procedures:

- Conceptual design
- Design development: floor plans or presentations
- Color consultations
- Creative problem-solving
- Implementing painting or wallpapering projects
- Working with dealers to procure home furnishings or accessories
- Hiring and managing craftsmen and contractors
- Order purchasing and processing
- Receiving, delivery, and installations

Because there aren't any strict guidelines for what a residential designer will and will not do, designers may be asked to stretch their range of services to accommodate a high-profile client. Designers have to use their own judgment in order not to compromise their set of business principles.

Don't be fooled: Residential design is not all about nurturing client relationships and building collective visions. That is actually the fun part. Establishing and sticking to a project budget can be as painless, or painful, as you and your client make it. As in life, when dollars come into play, claws may come out even in the best working relationships.

Young designers in particular must be savvy when establishing a budget that satisfies the client's and the designer's bottom line. Regardless of how much money a client has in the bank, no one wants to spend resources they aren't required to spend. In the early part of a career, young designers will surely run into cheap clients who desperately want a designer home on a discount budget. In these situations, we advise you to run for the hills.

Discount Magic Kills the Bottom Line

For more on client budgeting, we highly suggest you read chapter 11, "Client Management." But in the meantime, steer clear of clients who ask you to "work your discount magic" to swing better deals for them across the board. Remember, the client is the one with the money! If a client repeatedly asks you to go on eBay to find deals (rather than shop at showrooms) or use your designer discount to cut deals with manufacturers, wholesalers, or contract workers, the money you save for your client almost always comes out of your (or your supplier's) pocket.

Do we need to remind you that reducing your profit margin is not good business? Residential designers must have a firm understanding of the business as well as their own skills set in order to know what realistically can be done within a client's budgetary limitations. Think long and hard before you cut your profit margin in order to keep a client happy. If you give in to these spendthrifts even once, you risk opening the floodgates to a sea of red ink that will drown your bottom line and eventually your business.

As you can see, people skills, business acumen, flexible strength, and creative savvy are some of the keys to success in the residential design field. But that doesn't mean there is a master blueprint for success. Residential designers are often hired to analyze an individual's living situation and come to a unique set of design conclusions that may never be replicated in any of their future projects. It's true: No two residential clients or spaces are alike. The same cannot be said for businesses and non residential design.

NON RESIDENTIAL OR COMMERCIAL DESIGN

We aren't here to disparage the field of commercial design, but if you're interested in pursuing a career in this segment, you shouldn't be surprised to learn that corporate design work is a far less personal endeavor than residential design. That's not to say that the human touches are not important, as most businesses these days understand the importance of creating a working environment that is comfortable and conducive to doing good work, attracting clients, and retaining employees.

In some circles, however, commercial design work is considered contract work. Call it what you will, but know that these working relationships are almost always very formal and businesslike in nature. Commercial projects can vary from designing business offices, restaurants, hotels, and retail stores to schools, retirement communities, theaters, and nightclubs.

Non residential work is probably the most competitive segment in the design world because, rather than an individual client hiring a residential designer, a design firm will often bid or compete for a commercial project. When taking on a non residential project, you're not designing for an individual or a family; you are designing for a group whose employees and clients must feel alert, professional, and productive. Organization and efficiency are essential.

Bottom-line success factors in designing for the non residential segment are organization in budgeting and planning, efficiency in interactions with corporate clients, efficiency in space management, and the ability to create designs that can be renewed over a span of years. Most commercial clients aren't interested in remodeling their workspace every year, or even every five years, so be prepared to develop design schemes that span the test of time.

Know Your Audience

Not only are corporate designs prone to a more businesslike look and feel, but it is also imperative that your working relationships be less personal and more formal than they would be in residential design. You must be prepared to work within the parameters of your clients' corporate culture, and should learn to speak their language.

To land a commercial project, you must exude the personality of the business. This means you have to know your audience. If you are pitching a design proposal to a conservative office full of accountants, don't show up in a flashy outfit and pitch a trendy design concept. Know that when some members of the corporate sector think of "designers," they automatically think of overpriced divas with inflated egos. Prospective clients will be observing your business tactics from the very start, so don't go in unprepared and with an uninspired vision. Use your people skills to read your audience.

Once you're in the game, you must have a sophisticated approach to the bidding process in order to accurately gauge a prospective client's needs and—most important for the corporate sector—estimate the overall cost.

Remember, commercial designers, in your haste to land the client, don't forget to account for how you are going to make a profit on the endeavor. Capitalism is not evil! As they say in corporate America, CYA—cover your a—. Dot your i's, straighten your tie, and slip into a conservative Brooks Brothers suit so they know you are, at least for the duration of the project, one of them.

Nothing for Free

Be extremely careful not to spend too much time "off the clock" developing a plan for a company whose leaders aren't certain they want to spend the necessary money to redesign their space. Commercial accounts are notorious for wanting a lot of work up front before any money changes hands. The first red flag should go up when a prospective client isn't willing to compensate you, at least nominally, for your consultation work.

Scores of naïve designers have spent wasted hours building a comprehensive vision for a prospective nonresidential client, only to find the project cancelled due to lack of will, time, or resources. As they say on Wall Street, "Business is business," and so, when a company's third quarter earnings come out and its stock is underperforming, guess what gets trimmed from the budget? You.

Additional Thoughts on Commercial Design

Here are some other factors to consider in weighing the pros and cons of non residential design:

- Commercial offices are expensive to open and operate.
- Commercial design requires extensive code and licensing requirements.
- Commercial equipment costs a significant amount, and staffing requirements are significant.
- When compared to residential design, commercial design tends to be relatively generic in scope.
- A committee, rather than an owner, often makes the commercial design decisions.

- In most instances, on a square-foot basis as well as by the hour, compensation in the residential segment far outstrips that of the commercial segment.

- Even in hotels, country clubs, and retirement communities, the budget generally dictates what gets done and when.

- Many residential jobs take many months to complete, while commercial projects can go on for what seems like forever.

- The personal relationship with commercial clients is generally less rewarding than it is with residential clients.

CASE STUDY: AUER DESIGN ASSOCIATES

We've talked about residential interior design and how our passion for that segment of the business keeps us engaged and busy. What about those designers with a passion for commercial design? Don't they have something to say about the state of the business? Oh, yes; and for that, we've contacted another member of our professional group to give us her perspective. Now it's time to hear from a commercial interior design professional.

Debra Auer, of Auer Design Associates, is a Chicago, Illinois–based interior designer with over twenty-five years of experience. Debra was educated at Ferris State University, in the Kendall College of Art and Design. Today Debra has an established reputation for the intelligent integration of architecture and interior design. She has completed projects throughout the nation. Debra's design philosophy features a refined use of materials, sophisticated color, and sensitivity to scale.

A Passion for Commercial Design

While at Ferris State University, I found there were no commercial interior design classes offered, yet I knew from the beginning that I wanted to be involved in commercial design. After graduating, my first job experience was with a furniture dealer whose major clients were in the health care market. Having already identified a preference for commercial projects, I attended continuing education classes as part of the Harvard Professional Development program, dealing with different approaches to retirement housing, assisted living, and people with Alzheimer's. I also made a point of attending the yearly national symposium on health care design.

For the past twenty years, I have worked primarily in the commercial realm with an emphasis on senior living and health care. Commercial design appeals to me for multiple reasons, but I mainly enjoy the wide variety of project types and challenges. Health care projects may contain aspects such as the control of infectious diseases and unique life safety issues that need to be addressed along with aesthetic design decisions. Senior housing allows the incorporation of different aspects of hospitality, health care, and residential design, which to me is the best of both worlds.

In my opinion, working on commercial interiors has allowed me to work on projects of a larger scope and a more diverse nature than a typical residential practice might afford. My largest project to date was on a new women's hospital with over 938,000 square feet. In my experience, identifying the decision makers within commercial markets such as health care may be complex, because commercial work often requires the designer to interact with committees of multiple people with varying opinions. This might possibly be the greatest challenge facing me as a designer, as it is my role to consider all the factors present and try to reach a consensus with those committees and opinions.

Alone or in a Crowd

I have worked as a sole practitioner and as part of one of the larger architectural design firms in Chicago. Each experience has had its benefits. Working as part of a large design team was a wonderful learning experience and allowed me to work on projects of a larger scale with greater diversity and complexity. A smaller design team, on the other hand, can provide a greater sense of ownership and responsibility. Still, the best feeling for me comes as the result of a completed project, dreams realized, and a proud client.

Working in the senior living market segment has allowed me to draw from my experiences in health care, hospitality, residential, and facility work. My goal is to provide a creative environment that is supportive and enhances the quality of life for the residents and the caregivers.

While basic design issues may be common to both residential and commercial design practices, one of the primary technical differences between them is the importance of life safety and building code issues. Health care projects often require interaction with state and local health departments, which can greatly influence design direction. Stylistically, an eclectic approach seems to work best with my commercial projects. The ability to work within multiple approaches allows me flexibility that can be of value in dealing with all of the variables present in commercial interior design. While my primary market concentration is in the health care design realm, my experience in working on various commercial projects and a variety of project types has proven more economically viable, providing project diversity in times of change.

A Pearl Beyond Price

One of the more common issues commercial designers face is simply not understanding the intent and goals of their client. Some designers I've met tend to concentrate, instead, on fitting the project to the design idea. My intent is to combine contemporary and traditional elements into timeless environments.

The constant is extraordinary attention to detail. I believe a designer's primary focus is providing clients with an interior that reflects their needs, originality, and expectations. Knowing that I have created an environment that enhances the quality of someone's life is priceless to me.

PRODUCT DESIGN

Now that you've read our take on residential versus non residential design, let's discuss another design segment that has exploded in popularity in recent years—the business of product design.

The term "product design" covers the design, manufacture, and distribution of a custom-made product line. Products range from textiles, bedding, and wallpaper to accessories, furniture, and window treatments. Custom-made product lines usually come to life when an enterprising designer with plenty of capital sees a need in the marketplace for a product that does not yet exist.

Say a designer has an environmentally conscious client who wants to design a stylish yet eco-friendly space. The client wants every product, fabric, furniture, and accessory in the space to be "green," or not harmful to the environment. Working within the constraints of the client vision, a designer begins sourcing green products.

While on the hunt, the designer may decide he or she wants to place organic damask wallpaper in the space. But does a green line of damask wallpaper even exist? If a designer can't source it, he or she may choose to create one.

Truth be told, designers have been custom-making products for eons. Due to the fact that so many spaces are unique, interior designers are often frustrated by their inability to find a piece that fits and are forced to modify or custom-make products.

Twenty years ago, a client or designer probably would not have envisioned a hemp-damask wallpaper line, but in the specialized world we live in today, anything is possible. And in the opinion of many clients, everything should be available. After all, high-end clients aren't used to buying off the rack, so they often aren't shy about customizing virtually everything in their home if it suits their needs and their budget.

From the perspective of two interior designers, of course we believe it's possible to make the leap from designing interiors to product design. Our rationale is that interior designers are in a prime position to realize a need in the marketplace and then produce a product that fills that void. Many designers have what it takes to move into the product design world simply because they were taught in school to design graphics, create fabrics, and even build furniture.

On the other hand, a product designer may not have the education or design tools necessary to transition successfully into interior design, much in the same way that an architect's degree would not allow a seamless transition to designing interiors. They are indeed distinct disciplines.

If you are a design-minded individual who sees a need in the marketplace for a particular product and has a vision and the resources to make it a reality, by all means, give it a shot. Today, hundreds if not thousands of specialty product designers are thriving on the latest trend: furnishing spaces with custom-made goods. Why not you? It's all about finding a demand for a product that has yet to be met in the marketplace, and then meeting it.

DESIGNING WITHIN A RETAIL ENVIRONMENT

Some entrepreneurs in the marketplace prefer to operate hybrid businesses in which they hang an interior design shingle inside a retail shop. These retail designers have adopted the model shared by individual designers like Rose Cumming and large department stores like Harrods, Bloomingdale's, and Harvey Nichols that began offering in-house interior design services to customers more than one hundred years ago. In our humble opinion, this one-stop-shop business model is the worst of the five design segments.

In the best-case scenario, the two divisions of the business complement each other in perfect symbiosis. In the worst-case scenario, the combination of businesses does more harm than good. This rings especially true for small businesses that do not have the operating capital of a large corporation like Bloomingdale's. Let us count the ways that such a match made in heaven can turn into a marriage from hell:

- Retail design businesses require two different sets of staff.
- Retail design businesses require two different sets of business acumen.
- Retail design businesses require two different business spaces (a retail space and a designer office).
- Retail management is different from design office management.
- For retail designers, the hours of operation are usually very long.
- Inventory costs tie up huge amounts of cash, which cut into the overall profitability of any firm where interior design and retail inventories are combined.

In retail design, profits from merchandise sales almost always surpass the income made from interior design services. This is not to say that all designers working in retail stores are token designers, but the truth is that many store owners throw in free design consultations and services with the purchase of large orders in order to sweeten the deal for preferred customers.

Regardless of how important you feel it is to make a living strictly as a designer and not as a hybrid salesperson, if you choose retail design, you will be working with a limited palette. This means your design visions will likely be restricted to the confines of the retail store. Rarely are retail designers given the freedom to "think outside the box" by outsourcing furniture, fabrics, or accessories from other establishments if a perfectly suitable option is already on the shelf at their store.

If you are interested in pursuing what is, in our opinion, a high-risk, low-reward venture, at the very least, you should create two profit centers (one for the retail business and one for the design business) and monitor overtime, which proves to be the most advantageous to your bottom line. If you find the hybrid approach works for you, bravo! If you find the hybrid approach works for the shop owner but *not* for you as a designer, then by all means move on to something else. Life is too short not to.

ARCHITECTURAL DESIGN

With so many years of experience in the industry, we've seen just about every Tom, Dick, and Harry throw his hat into the design ring at one time or another. That's capitalism—with increased consumer demand comes more suppliers, some of whom have a genuine passion for design and others who are in it not for the love of design but for less altruistic motives like the lure of hot cash.

Yes, we're alluding to architecture firms. If you haven't deduced it, we have a strong opinion about architects. Are they hacks? Not necessarily; but, as professional designers, we worry that the work coming out of these large offices isn't necessarily of the best quality. Equally troubling is the fact that unless you're working for an architecture firm, these architectural designers are taking business away from you as an individual designer.

Intrusion into the Design Industry

It's undeniable: The architectural designer's extension into interior design has made a huge splash in the design pool due to the sheer number of jobs full-service firms (which handle architecture *and* interior design) are able to acquire. Like all businesses, architectural firms are looking for any way to increase their profitability. Adding an interior design division adds a profit center to the business and keeps the architect in the driver's seat of any project.

When considering the pros and cons of architectural design, let's begin with the fact that most architects are not schooled in the basics of interior design. Many architects come to interior design with what they believe is a God-given right.

Candidly speaking, most architects look down on interior designers as unworthy and unprofessional. Architects tend to be arrogant, conservative, unimaginative, and very tightly bound. From the architects' point of view, branching out their business keeps all aspects of a job in-house and easy to manage. Most architects would argue that this kind of diversification keeps their vision of a project intact.

The Value of a Second Opinion

We believe there is nothing wrong with having a "fresh eye" on a project. This is not to second-guess the architect, but to review what is happening with a professional and unbiased eye. In our experience, the interior designer brings a feel for the project that is slightly more in sync with the client and not so controlled by the architect. Architects can be very controlling and, truth be told, some (of course, not all) architecture firms are operated like mini-dictatorships, where any ideas that run counter to the architect's vision are strictly verboten.

If one were so inclined, one might compare architecture/design firms to mini-monopolies that added design to their already lucrative business model in order to take clients on a "one-stop-shop ride" from a building's inception to its birth. We aren't so bold as to connect those dots but, after reading this chapter, you certainly may.

Our firm has caught many would-be mistakes while going over what were meant to be final architectural drawings for construction. In one instance, we inexplicably found a family room that was only going to be eight-and-one-half feet wide by eighteen feet long! The client hadn't realized the problem, and the architect never confessed to the mistake even though it was right there on the plans. The architect called it an "in-house" mistake but, had construction begun, it would have been costly for someone—most likely, not the architect. This reinforces the value of getting a fresh perspective on a design project.

Other Considerations

Architectural firms are also notorious "old boys' clubs," which means they've been known to overlook women for promotions and relegate them to staff positions. Another problem that arises between architects and interior designers is that most architects see no real value (beyond profit) in interior design and, therefore, view both their male and female interior design employees as minions.

In evaluating whether the architectural design segment is for you, remember who you are and what you do best. If you're an architect with an interest in building your skills to include interior design, this segment is right up your alley. Conversely, if you're a designer unfamiliar with the business of architecture, it may be extremely difficult to prosper in this segment.

We believe education and experience are of the utmost importance for a young designer. If you are offered a job in the design section of an architectural firm, if it fits with your career path, we suggest that you take it. That said, be very careful about how long you stay at an architectural firm. Don't let the grass grow under your feet!

CASE STUDY: THE TROUBLE WITH ARCHITECTS

Of course, we know there are talented architectural designers out there; in our opinion, they are just few and far between. Our main complaint with architects is the control factor. We can't tell you how many times in our careers we've heard of architects bullying homeowners into designs that fit the architects' blueprints but not the true visions of the clients. Many architects are under the opinion that "architects know best," and some-times, especially when it comes to designing structures, they do. But when it comes to designing interiors, shouldn't the client at least have a say in the matter?

Here's a real-life example: For a number of years, we worked with a client in Pebble Beach. She consistently exuded taste, selecting the best of fabrics for drapery, furniture, and furnishings. We felt we had her trust because she always praised what we'd done for her. When we heard she was thinking of renovating her more modest home to add more space and create a new exterior, we assured her we would be happy to work on the project.

Then, unknown to us, she contacted a local architect and asked him to draw up plans. Only after the plans were ready did she give us a call, and we were thunderstruck. The architect had proposed to do all the construction management, the interior design, and all the other details. The client felt compelled to go with his plan even though some aspects of the project were not to her liking. For us, all seemed lost.

Then the client bought a pickup truck for towing her horse trailer. She con-sequently wanted to change the plan the architecture firm had proposed by adding a new garage. But the architect wouldn't have any of it and told her that she would take his plan as it was or not at all. Fortunately, she had not signed a contract. She gave us a call and asked for our input. We suggested bringing in our strategic partner, a building firm, to consult on plans we would prepare. The upshot was a complete renovation based on our plans for the space.

This experience helped us learn to always let clients know the range of our expertise and strategic partnerships. With our lesson learned, we have gone on to manage a number of projects from inception to completion. Turning the tables to our advantage has put us in the driver's seat for most projects while making our time and sales much more profitable.

Today, through project managing building firms, we essentially accomplish exactly what architecture firms do. Our partners are happy to receive our business and design blueprints molded to fit the true visions of our clients.

FINAL THOUGHTS ON CHOOSING A DESIGN SEGMENT

Understanding your place in the interior design business doesn't just happen overnight. It requires a lot of planning, as well as knowing yourself and where you want your future to take you. A sense of direction is extremely important, so don't take it lightly. Think about it, study the options, meditate, and ask established designers their opinion.

We truly believe it's best to focus on one design segment—residential design, commercial design, product design, designing within a retail environment, or architectural design—at the beginning of your career, while being sure not to limit yourself. You can always evolve your business plan to move into other areas of design. So, pick a design segment and become an expert. Try out different areas or dabble in every segment while continuing to focus on your area of choice.

For many designers, commercial design may be the best track, even with its more stringent code requirements and its competitive marketplace. For others, the residential segment may be for you because of its accessibility to new designers just entering the marketplace.

Should you decide to open a hybrid retail shop or start a firm that has a residential and a commercial division, be sure to create two separate profit centers and segment out the design work, profits, costs, and sales in order to get an objective viewpoint. Then, over a period of time, ascertain which is most profitable.

You may decide to separate the businesses or even to close one. As with so many things in life, as you become proficient in one area, the other areas may not interest you as much as they did when you were just starting out.

PLUNGING OFF THE DESIGNER HIGH DIVE

On Starting Your Own Business

"The idea of starting your own firm is exciting, but
there is no point in starting it if you do not intend to
make it a success."

—MARY V. KNACKSTEDT

Congratulations, neophytes—with a more holistic understanding of the
design industry and a sharper sense of the opportunities and obstacles
young designers face in the early part of their careers, you're already better
equipped to meet your destiny. Now let's put the pedal to the metal (shall
we?) and shift our discussion from advising junior designers on how to
"cut their teeth" in the real world to mentoring budding visionaries who
are itching to take a daring leap into the world of entrepreneurial design.

BUILDING YOUR OWN YELLOW BRICK ROAD

Surely we're not the first to tell you that meeting your destiny halfway will
only get you so far in this crazy world. As with so many life endeavors,
"destiny" is an open-ended prospect that is what you make it, particularly
in the ultra-competitive design arena. Understanding that there are only
so many seats at the designer table, each of you should brace for the possibility that you may not be met halfway or have the "yellow brick road"
to success laid out for you. You must be prepared to pave your own road.
After all, that's what we did.

To some, that this may sound daunting, while to others, the limitless
possibility of literally designing your own career path from its foundation
is a thrilling prospect. For those of you who are currently feeling that
tingly entrepreneurial sensation, this chapter and the rest of this book are
for you.

65

Holistically speaking, it's no surprise that so many designers dream of one day running their own show. After all, what is interior design all about if not building a vision from the ground up? Indeed, many of today's design entrepreneurs are born as much as they are made. Go ahead—ask around your nearest design center, and you'll find that most of us simply can't help "doing what we do."

Mutuality aside, that doesn't mean we're all meant to run a business. We are all wired very differently; just look at our discrepant design tastes! Some designers are more comfortable working for others their entire careers, and these situations fit well for some people. No industry would function without foot soldiers and lieutenants. But we—and many like us—are never happy being someone else's foot soldiers.

Try asking yourself, What type of designer am I? Here's a tip: If you were born with the entrepreneurial gene, you probably already know. Its fire tends to burn within from an early age. We learned early on that to succeed on your own in this business, you have to give it all you've got. Failure must always be a prescient consideration, but never an option. So for us, despite the fact that we were fairly inexperienced young designers, it was just a matter of when and how. We were diving in off the high dive.

For those of you who are still on the fence about being an entrepreneurial designer, our mission is to get you closer to one side or another by unveiling a handy questionnaire we call the Hale-Williams Entrepreneurial Test. Give it a whirl; we think it will do wonders for your confidence by giving you a more holistic understanding of your fears and desires. Ready, set, grow!

THE HALE-WILLIAMS ENTREPRENEURIAL TEST

Let's say you're a young, talented designer who can boast sky-high ambition, solid financing, and an out-of-this-world business model or product design idea. You want to enter the design business not as someone else's design assistant, but as the proprietor of your own practice. We think that's phenomenal and wish you the best of luck. Just one question: Do you realize that running a business is the design equivalent of walking a tightrope without a net? We hope you've got some cushion if you fall.

We've compiled twelve broad questions to help you determine whether or not you're ready to start your own design business.

Question 1: Can You Beat the Odds?
Nine out of ten interior designers agree that right out of the design chute, young entrepreneurs will have the toughest time with the following real-world factors:

- Generating the capital to start a business
- Knowing what kind of business you want to operate
- Building a winning business model
- Knowing the type of clients you want to attract
- Attracting clients
- Knowing how to run a business

If being an entrepreneur sounds like a gamble, that's because it is. Starting your own business is likely to be the biggest risk of your life. If you "deal yourself in" too soon at the professional designer's table, you'd better have a few aces up your sleeve. Straight shooters in the design community will tell you that only one in five hundred designers coming out of design school has what it takes to build a successful practice.

But that doesn't mean some of you riverboat gamblers can't beat the odds. After all, you're you! The world has never seen anyone like you, right? So, put your poker face on and get confident, because if you don't believe, no one will.

To "make it" as an entrepreneur, you have to be confident that you will stand out in an arena full of proud peacocks and daring design divas. How do we know? We're living proof! We're two regular guys who "did it our way" largely because we didn't believe all the naysayers. We believed in ourselves and had the benefit of two intangible factors on our side. The question is: Do you have them, too?

Question 2: Do You Have the Two Intangible Factors?

Much of your success as a design entrepreneur will hinge on whether or not you can tap into two powerful, sometimes magical forces. What are these two factors? We're going to tell you.

The first entrepreneurial intangible is the "it" factor. Whether a new designer has "it" or not will play an enormous role in the success of his or her career. Not only does a designer's "it" factor attract clients and generate good buzz; the power of "it" often starts the branding process for a designer's burgeoning business. Like a film director with a signature style, a designer's "it" factor can be a calling card that's the ticket to name recognition in this industry. But what is "it," really?

Everyone has a different opinion, but we see "it" as a blend of blinding design talent, supernatural charm, and unbending intent. A potent dose of "it" in the right industry places can literally turn a hot "it" girl with taste into a hot "it" designer on the scene. It sounds like a fairy tale, but such stories actually happen.

If any of you are packing a strong "it" factor in your designer suitcase, you're already light years ahead of the pack. Why? Because so many in our industry clearly do not have "it." You may not be able to describe your own professional mojo to a tee (yet), but trust us: Clients know when they see it. So, believe in yourself and strut your "it" factor for anyone who will listen. Maybe one day you'll become an "it" designer overnight. How badly do you want "it"?

Once you wake from your designer daydream, know that only a narcissistic celebutante would start a business based on "it" factor alone. There is another intangible factor that's just as important: Will you shrivel up and die if you don't become a designer? If you answer *Yes* to that question, you may be in the right classroom.

In anything you do, your desire to succeed must be on par with your talent, business acumen, and charisma. This means that if you're not tenacious in this industry, you're not trying hard enough.

Just ask any entrepreneurial designer about what it takes to be successful in the competitive side of the business, and watch a seemingly nice, sweet-talking person turn into a pit bull in sheep's clothing. If you don't believe us, then you don't know many entrepreneurial designers.

Question 3: Do You Live to Work?

So which is it: Do you "work to live," or do you "live to work"? We know this question has become a cliché, but it also happens to be an apt inquiry at this point, so humor us by deciding which answer best fits your personality. If you find you're the type of person who "works to live," you may want to put down this book, take a hard look in the mirror, and decide if running a business is really for you.

Proprietorship is not a nine-to-five job; it is a life endeavor. Learn it, live it...love it. The quicker you accept or reject this notion, the better. We sincerely hope each of you has come to our "paperback symposium" with a burning desire to "live your work," almost to the point of obsession. That's right, we said *obsession*.

A burning passion for your business will help you in every way. When we began our careers, we lived our work to the point of obsession. It flowed into every facet of our lives, and it paid off handsomely for us. That's why we truly believe that without embodying the "live to work" ethic in our early years, we wouldn't have been nearly as successful as we are today.

Now, after a few hundred major successes, we are able to live to work so we can live, while the joy we get from running a business continues to flow into every facet of our lives. Now we love every minute of it.

Question 4: Your Business or Your Life?

We hear what some of you are saying: "I'm a born workaholic, but that doesn't mean I want to remain one for the rest of my life." We say, Who does? But one of the fundamental things one must understand (and accept) about the lifelong challenge ahead is how much time it's actually going to take to get your business off the ground.

No designer on earth would be able to sustain eighty-hour workweeks for the duration of a career, but you'd better believe you will be working heavy hours in your early years, or you'll never get established. You've got to want it more than the rest, remember?

As an entrepreneur, your business is your life, especially in the beginning. It is a lifestyle as much as it is a profession, and if you do it right, you'll find that the line is quickly blurred between the "real you" and the "entrepreneurial you." If that is a frightening notion, you might want to reconsider entrepreneurship.

Question 5: Do You Do Residential?

As you know, we believe it's more realistic for a young design graduate to start his or her own residential practice because of the opportunities to get in the game. If you need a refresher, check out the inherent perks that come with starting a residential practice, and then tell us whether or not you're interested:

- The capital investment in starting a residential design business is relatively low.
- Residential designers can start out working from a home office.
- Word of mouth works better in residential design than in any other design sector.
- More money can be made in residential design than in other fields of design.
- Residential designers only have to sell their skills to a select number of clients.
- It's relatively easy to establish clientele through networking, social settings, and professional events.

Question 6: Do You Have a Twelve-Month Cushion?

Besides residential design, young entrepreneurs have also been known to dive into product design right out of the gate. This is a wonderful choice if the designer has a great product, furniture, or accessory idea and the resources to turn a dream into reality.

But here's the hard part: Regardless of what segment of the industry they choose, young designers starting their own businesses shouldn't risk it unless they're able to support themselves for the first twelve months with no income. That is not a misprint. In this day and age, young entrepreneurs need twelve months of cushion—no kidding. As with any business, you have to understand that you aren't going to take every job that comes along. This means you have to be able to live through the rough times in the beginning, hence the need for a cushion. Are you still interested in starting your own business?

Question 7: Do You Know What Drives You?

As we discussed, it's essential that young designers find out what they do best as early in their career as possible. If you're truly serious about starting a practice, you absolutely, positively have to know what you do best, because your livelihood and reputation are both at stake.

One problem is that there are so many different roads to explore. Another is that once you decide on a path, there are so many different levels of clientele you can target with your services. You can start by identifying what segment of the industry you want to revolutionize. Is it residential, commercial, architecture, retail, or product design? Once you've identified your segment of choice, keep drilling, because the questions keep getting deeper:

- If you're into commercial design, are you into health care, corporate, or hospitality?

- If you're into residential design, are you into kitchen and bath, or lighting?

- If you're into product design, are you planning a furniture, textile, or accessory line?

- If you're into retail design, is it as a shopkeeper, a retail store designer, or a furniture store designer?

These are merely a few of the potential questions you will have to ask yourself. There are so many possibilities for just one life. While you are in the process of exploring the specialty segments that may or may not work for you, don't do anything drastic like open a business. It behooves you to first know what you do best. Then, after you've figured it out, you can begin building a business plan that best suits your skill set. Makes sense, right? Of course it does!

Question 8: Do You Specialize?

With design specialization being "so hot right now," many of you aspiring entrepreneurs may be moved to master one of our industry's niche segments in order to establish yourselves as fresh up-and-comers in the design community. It's a wonderful way to get a foot in the door. Don't be afraid to specialize early, especially if a great opportunity comes your way.

Go ahead: design a kitchen one week and a furniture line the next. Who knows—many young designers find so much work focusing on a particular specialty area that they are inspired to start a specialty design business. So, how does one become a multi dimensional designer? As you try your hand at a few of the specialty segments, don't forget to start developing a signature style you do well while not letting it limit your overall scope. Instead, use your experience as a building block to the next challenge.

Expand your mind by "doing it all," and feel free to be a specialist for a day in any area you like. This exercise will help you "connect the dots" in your career by coming to new realizations about yourself.

Say you're a young designer who discovers "functional design" is your "thing." That's great—functional design is very "in" right now, but can you connect the dots by, for example, building your love of function into a business plan? Start by identifying an audience that needs functionally designed spaces.

An immediate idea would be to start an urban residential or corporate commercial practice, due to the large role function plays in those two segments. This is not a bad notion, but an inspired thought would be to start a business that specializes in retirement communities and spaces for disabled clients. It may not exactly be the most glamorous design niche there is, but it is a profitable one that's a great example of connect the dots thinking by a designer with an eye on the prize.

While you're in this self-exploration phase, we hope you can appreciate how far you've already come. The beauty of this industry is there are no rules. Your goal in experimenting is to layer your skills so you and your future business aren't one-dimensional. Then, once you have a wide-ranging skill set, you can either choose to specialize in one area or work in multiple design mediums.

It's entirely up to you, but when it comes to opening a business, you'd better get it right the first time, or that shingle you hang out will come down awfully quickly.

Question 9: Who Is Your Audience?

No matter what kind of innovative product or service you have percolating in your design cooker, the fact is that it's not going to fly in the business world unless quite a few people buy into it. This is particularly true in the design arena, where it's virtually impossible to go the undiscovered genius route. We all must be appreciated and compensated in our time.

Every successful designer (and design business) must have a paying audience, so who is your target market? If you are at a loss, perhaps you should consider holding off on the whole "starting a business" thing until you're a bit more prepared. The bottom line is that no savvy designer goes into business without knowing his or her audience.

Try going back to "Understanding the Modern Client" in chapter 2, and ask yourself, If I were to start a business, would I be selling to typical modern clients (who are young, urban, and into functional spaces) or am I more interested in attracting affluent clients with my "it" factor and my grand ideas? Until you know what type of client you want to secure, you don't know anything.

Question 10: What's the Worst That Can Happen?

A huge factor in your decision is determining the level of risk you are comfortable taking at this point in your career. For some people, starting a business is just not realistic. Life, in the shape of a family and a mortgage, has a funny way of sidetracking some of our grandest dreams. While a young, single designer with no dependents may be more inclined to throw caution to the wind and start a design firm, a designer who is a single mother with three kids may not be in the same position because she has so much more to lose.

As for you, make some time to deal honestly with your entrepreneurial fears and desires. Try taking a personal inventory to see where you stand. Here are a few questions that will help you to determine whether you're in the right place to start your own business:

- What are your responsibilities? Do you have a family, kids, or a mortgage?
- How is your credit? Do you already have significant debt?
- What's the worst that can happen if you fail?
- Do you have a backup plan?
- Are you going to "die" if you don't start your own practice?
- Do you plan to run your business as a business or a hobby?
- Are you self-motivated? Can you start a job and finish it?

Question 11: Do You Have Clarity of Thought?

One of the keys to running any successful business is being able to maintain a clear thought process at all times. This may look easy from the sidelines, but in the heat of battle you will find it harder than you think.

Clarity of mind (and its partner, clarity of action) will help you at every step in your design career. From objectively seeing when a job has been done right or wrong to knowing when to bring in outside help to improve business, a sharp eye and a sharper mind are two crucial designer attributes that will never, ever go out of style.

However, contrary to what some of your professors may have told you, success isn't determined by how many attributes you have on your dossier. It is more mysterious than that. Of all the intangible factors out there, the four that will weigh heaviest in the early part of your career are: staying sharp, being resourceful, playing to your strengths, and knowing how to compensate for your weaknesses. You need to know your game better than anyone else does.

How do you go about doing all this? Begin by developing the clarity of mind to see what you do well and what needs work. Once you know the holes in your game, you can address them through self-improvement or by partnering with other design specialists who are experts in areas that you are not.

For example, if you find you aren't very good at organization, partner with someone who is. If you can see you're having problems with color, bring in a color specialist. If you're a control freak, learn to delegate. This is, frankly, the reason so many designers go the partnership route. Smart designers are aware of their limitations before starting their practice. They know that to succeed, their businesses must be able to do it all, even if they cannot do it all individually.

Question 12: Got Any Street Smarts, Wise Guy?

Say you're a gutsy designer determined to go into business right out of school. That's fantastic, but we hope you weren't brainwashed by your professors into thinking that your business is going to be run "by the book," because here in the real world, it usually doesn't work that way.

Even if doing it "by the books" has gotten you everywhere in your nascent career, when it comes to becoming a professional designer, an over-reliance on education can lead to your demise. At least in our industry, strict academic types tend to be stiff in spirit and unable to create, improvise, and invent on the fly—all fairly giant factors in what we do. Does this mean these designers weren't talented when they entered school, or did education somehow play a part in their creative demise? It may be a combination of the two as, in this day and age, it's all too easy for anyone to enroll in a design school, pass a series of tests, and still not be any closer to being a qualified or even talented designer. There is a reason that some of the greatest designers never went to design school. A tightly wound internal curriculum can kill a designer's creative spark.

We aren't saying education is useless. A solid foundation is important in any career. But let's face it, design degrees can be very misleading. And there are quite a few nasty habits that some students learn in design school. Let's just say that when it comes to the practice of interior design, what often happens in the classroom should stay in the classroom.

If you want an example, take a look at the architecture industry. They've gone down this slippery slope. The people you meet in architecture today are often conventional and unimaginative. Because of the industry's tightly bound curriculum, you meet many young architects who have had all their creativity sucked out of them. They simply learned a regimented profession by rote over five years and passed the test. How is this a paradigm for success? The textbook answer: it isn't.

FINAL THOUGHTS ON TAKING THE PLUNGE

We hope our little exercise was as good for you as it was for us. If you responded positively to the twelve entrepreneurial questions presented above, you're well on your way to knowing whether you have what it takes to start your own design business.

Your goal now should be to keep exploring and keep digging—be relentless in your search. Now that you have a better understanding of some of the intangibles that go into being an entrepreneur, with some hard work and a little luck, you can build your career to become anything you want.

Remember, interior design is still just a business. No great epiphanies will come while you sit on the fence. The more likely scenario is that after awhile, you will equivocate yourself into a state of permanent stasis. So, what are you waiting for? If you are a born entrepreneur who's ready to start your own practice, then go ahead and start it. Now is as good a time as any to take the leap. Like they say in the real estate industry, it doesn't matter how you get in or when you get in—just as long as you get in.

In today's market, even as a forty-year-old designer, you can create any kind of business you want, serve any kind of clientele you want, and use any pricing model you want. The key is to have unbending intent, which means having the courage to stand by your convictions.

Your Biggest Hurdle Is Fear

Starting a successful business is never easy; it has to be a labor of love. For most of us, there was a time early in our entrepreneurial careers when it could have gone either way. We could have dropped out and done something different, something easier. But we remained steadfast in our commitment to build our business, even when everyone else thought we should be "committed" to a loony bin.

As for your burgeoning career, we hate to tell you this, but you're going to have to find your own way. Nobody is going to give it to you. We survived to prosper in large part because of our "intangibles" and because we were mentally tough. You have to be strong, too, so toughen up and start tapping into your special blend of intangible "it" factors.

As you develop, the biggest challenge you will face will be to eliminate fear from your vocabulary. Have you noticed that the universe knows when you're afraid to take on challenges? Well, it does, so promise us that when it comes to starting a business, you won't ever walk away just because it's "not a good business to get into." Like everything in life, your business is the sum total of what you make it.

Your Mission, Should You Choose to Accept It

We've personally accomplished so many things we never dreamt were possible when we were twenty-five years old. We had no idea what we (or the world) would look like today. We thought we did, but we were wrong. So, when you're sitting in class talking about your future with your friends, all you twenty-five-year-old designers out there should realize that you haven't got a clue, either. Neither do you thirty-five-year-olds, for that matter.

The industry changes so fast; it's impossible to predict. Thus, one can only teach students so much. The meat of your knowledge will only come through experience in life, in work, in trial, and in error. Then, one bright day, you will look up and realize what you need to do to be successful.

Speaking of what you need to do, here's a refresher list for you aspiring entrepreneurs to take home and pin on your refrigerator:

- Educate yourself about the industry.
- Gain some real working experience.
- Discover what you do best.
- Try to connect the entrepreneurial dots.
- Establish yourself as a professional to build your reputation.
- Develop a business model around what you do best.
- Grow a team of business allies.
- Acquire the tools and resources you need to start a business.
- Open a design business.

In the "In" Crowd

This sounds like a cakewalk, doesn't it? Not exactly? Well, take comfort in the fact that the journey you're on to break into the industry—either as an interior designer or as a design entrepreneur—is a path you'll only have to take once. Because once you're in, you're *in*. It's like an entrepreneurial "snowball effect" that takes hold when the momentum you've established keeps your business going and growing. That's the day you realize that you will get more referrals from clients, that new clients will keep coming your way, and that you have become a successful design entrepreneur.

Once you're part of the designer "in" crowd in one of the large markets, you almost can't fail. This is from the standpoint that although your next project may not be all that exciting or glamorous, running a business is not about excitement or being a rock star. For most of us, it's about plying a trade, making money, and maintaining a level of clientele and style of service that suits your ambition. If you simply focus your attention on doing what you do well and making the profits you need to stay in business, you can run your business all day long. There is little mystery in how you breed that kind of success: It's called hard work, and it's been known to pay dividends from time to time.

But when the workday is through, guess what designers do to blow off steam? We talk—and we talk a lot. Translation: Everything you do, especially in the beginning of your career, will be observed and scrutinized by other designers. Take advantage of this inevitability by using it as an opportunity to gain exposure and build your reputation. You're going to find that most of your clients will be picked up either through networking with your connections or because of your hot new reputation around town. Flakey reputations just don't cut it anymore. So, get out there and show the world what you can do.

If You Do Decide to Take the Plunge

The good news is that you're diving into a neophyte industry that's still only beginning to understand its full potential. So, go ahead and build your vision; then, find a way to get there. And please don't just take our word for it. This is an enormous decision for you to make, so don't be capricious.

Read as many design books as you can get your hands on, talk to your loved ones, receive counsel from your mentors, and be absolutely certain before you dive in: your livelihood is at stake. In the coming chapters, we will go into more detail about what it really takes to start a design business, but for now, we'll leave you with a few entrepreneurial tips:

- Find an office away from home.
- Find a good lawyer and accountant.
- Stay out of debt as much as possible.
- Make sure you have a liquid cash reserve on hand.
- Don't forget to leave yourself open to new ideas and suggestions, even from a couple of old guys like us.

Now we sound like a couple of worried parents sending their kids off to camp! Get outta here and go have some fun.

CHAPTER 6

DEFINING YOUR DREAM

Understanding Models,
Pricing, and Fees

> "If I should fail in this life, let me
> at least fail at being me."
> —JODIE FOSTER

By now, most of you enterprising souls should know whether you're interested in practicing residential, commercial, retail, architectural, or product design. No pressure, but if you haven't decided, do some soul-searching and make certain, because that knowledge is going to come in handy now that we're ready to discuss how to build a business model for your design practice.

IF YOU BUILD IT

What is a business model? We're so glad you asked. Don't listen to what your catty designer "friends" tell you: a business model is no secret hand-shake; it's simply a means of defining how you do business and make money. It speaks to the very core of what you do as a designer. Call it what you will—a model, a plan, a blueprint—but think of yours as a conceptual tool that explains the business logic behind your design offering.

Virtually every designer who goes into business with no business model or plan for success crashes and burns royally. So, take it from two pros and don't be a royal flop out of the gate. Get in the game and decide on your segment.

Leaning on Our Residential Roots

When it comes to building your business plan, deciding on a segment is the first in a long line of questions that you must answer before you start thinking about opening your doors for business.

As you know, we at Hale-Williams are passionate about residential interior design. It's our lifeblood, and we sincerely hope it's in yours, too. (If anyone needs a refresher on why we believe residential is the best and most rewarding design segment, reread chapter 4, "Understanding Design Segments," to get caught up with the rest of the class.)

After hearing our take, if you still don't get our "residential drift," that's okay. We aren't going to think you're cheating on us. You have to follow your heart, and if it leads you to commercial, product, retail, or architectural design, that's fantastic. But be aware, disciples: In the coming pages we're going to lean heavily on our residential roots to teach you the fundamentals of business models, pricing, and fees. We hope you stick with us, because we've got a batch of lessons in the oven for entrepreneurs who are hungry for success.

Defining Your Business Model

Getting started is always the hardest part, so imagine you're building a road map to a unique concept that only you can see. Try defining all the moving parts that go into a successful business model, such as:

- Your design segment
- Your target market
- Your design product
- Your mission statement and philosophy
- Your business objectives

In identifying all the "moving parts" of your business as a young designer, you would be foolish not to reference what has worked for others. That is, after all, probably why you bought this book. Keep in mind that you do not have to bake your cake from scratch.

Whether you're looking to "go large" out of the gate by starting a design firm that employs three or more designers, or launch a boutique practice with two or fewer designers, get out there and study how successful designers in your segment make money. Talk to designers, seek out mentors, and find out how the good ones operate.

Look around and find other entrepreneurs who share your vision. How do they charge their clients? How do they form business partnerships? How do they operate? There are scores of winning tips out there that can creatively be incorporated into your plan if you're savvy. And for heaven's sake, don't limit your research to the design industry. A well-run business is a well-run business, no matter the type. Any tips from another occupation on how to get ahead can most likely be applied to what we do.

Opening Pandora's Box

Wake up, all you daydream believers! Just because you jotted down a mission statement and your design segment on a Starbucks napkin, don't run out and rent a design space just yet. We've only hit the tip of the iceberg. Like a Pandora's box of philosophical and tactical considerations, defining a business plan is a complex process that won't happen overnight. You have to put in the hard work.

All this "planning" (a four-letter word in many design circles) has been known to overwhelm those who haven't a clue as to how the industry works. This is because in addition to building a dynamic business product and a compelling design philosophy, a solid business model also includes how you:

- Bill for time
- Achieve profits
- Charge for goods
- File your taxes
- Compensate your employees
- Allocate money to pay overhead
- Purchase goods
- Run your office
- Charge your accounts
- Form business alliances
- Form business partnerships
- Send and receive invoices

The list goes on and on. For those who are looking for one key to success, keep looking. There is no magic bullet. Rather, there are hundreds of magic bullets that must be utilized and mastered. Somehow, they don't teach you that in design school, do they?

Are you up for the challenge? Remember, although you're developing nicely, you're still a beginner who is getting a holistic education on how to be an entrepreneur the right way. Let's continue to take it one step at a time, shall we?

Now that your eyes are open to the task at hand, we hope you won't mind if we break the modeling process down into a few digestible conversations. Before diving into tactical maneuvers like invoicing, ordering, receiving, and installing goods, we're going to focus on how to set up your business and start earning money by charging clients a fee. After all, hot cash is the oil in your engine, right? Money is certainly the means to your design ambitions and dreams.

Recruit Your Brain Trust

When money matters are concerned, always base your decisions on what your "brain trust" advises. Who the heck is your brain trust? We aren't talking about your roommate or your stylish mother; we mean every entrepreneur's safety net: a good accountant and an even better attorney. If you don't have one, go recruit your brain trust now or rue the day.

In selecting your two-headed council, it would be ideal if you could establish relationships with people who understand the design business. If you have industry friends, make some phone calls to find out which CPAs and lawyers other designers use. At a minimum, try to find an attorney who is competent and will answer the phone when you call. That's not a given in this world, and in this "rock-'em, sock-'em" business, you're going to need some on-the-spot advice at some point in your career. You just are.

HOW IS YOUR BUSINESS STRUCTURED?

Once you've established trusted council, one of the first jobs for your brain trust is determining the structure of your business. This is primarily for tax-filing purposes. Schedule a meeting, sit down with your brain trust, and lay it all out on the table—your business objectives, segment, product, target market, etc. Take a long, objective look at your goals and means (resources and capital). Let your brain trust help you determine which model is best for your situation. Listed below are some of the most popular options.

Popular Business Organizational Models

- Corporations—Incorporated (usually large) design or architecture firms that are separate legal entities from their members. If you want protection and have twenty or more employees, you may want to consider incorporating.

- S-corporations—S-corps work in some ways like sole proprietorships in that all the profits from the corporation are funneled to a sub-corporation, which is owned by one or more stakeholders who receive profits based on their slice of ownership. S-corps pay no taxes; the individual owners do.

- Limited liability companies—LLCs offer limited liability protection to their owners. Similar to corporations, LLCs provide a more flexible form of ownership, especially for smaller companies with a limited number of owners. If you have a small number of employees, you may want to consider an LLC.

- Partnerships—The Hale-Williams business model, in which two principal designers form a partnership in order to share the profits and/or losses of the business in which both are equally vested. A partnership may contain more than two members, and all are equally vested.

- Sole proprietorships—By far, the most popular model for young design entrepreneurs. In sole proprietorships, the designer does business in his or her own name. Legally, the business has no separate existence from its owner, which is the biggest downside. If there's any likelihood that you will be sued, and you have assets to protect, you may want to avoid this model. The liability limitations enjoyed by corporations or LLCs do not apply to sole proprietors.

- Cooperatives—A design cooperative is made up of several designers who share a common space but operate as independent contractors. Cooperatives are a great way for young designers to break into the industry, because they're often run by a senior designer (the official or unofficial principal) who rents space to junior designers.

Can you believe that Hale-Williams has employed each of these business models at one time or another? We don't know if that means we are business savvy, just getting old, or both. What we do know is that each incarnation was extremely important to us at a different time in our business lives.

We both started out as sole proprietors. Then, when we had staff in Baltimore, we felt it was important to be incorporated in the state of Maryland, so we became a corporation. After we moved to Carmel, we formed an LLC. Once we let go of our staff, we realized that we really didn't need to be an LLC anymore. So, we formed a partnership.

The lesson here is that there is no way we can logically tell you which way to go. It's up to you and your brain trust to decide. What we can say with confidence is that most young designers starting out form sole proprietorships and are just fine until they begin expanding, hiring employees, and forming partnerships with other designers.

CASE STUDY: TOM'S BUSINESS MODEL EDUCATION

When I (Tom) think back to how I came up with my first business model, I suppose my inspiration can be traced back to my entrepreneurial mother. Norma C. Williams was a costume designer back in my hometown of Memphis, Tennessee. Mom taught me so many valuable business lessons as a boy, successfully owning and operating her own business and retail shop for thirty-plus years. She was my template for success.

I didn't know it at the time, but I was soaking up entrepreneurial lessons like a sponge. Now I understand why I was so captivated with the way she did business. She was fabulous at what she did. I really wish she had charged more, but she made enough to send my brother and me to college, among other things. Here's how my mother's retail/costume design business model worked:

- She charged a fee for designing costumes.
- She charged a fee for producing costumes.
- She sold products (tap shoes, tights, leotards) at retail value out of her costume store.

A Three-Armed Profit Machine

As it turns out, my mother ran a retail, manufacturing, and service business all in one. The beauty was that each revenue stream or profit arm produced a profit that wasn't entirely dependent on the others. What a concept! What corresponding lessons did I apply to my design business? That's easy:

- I learned to diversify my business model by establishing more than one revenue stream or profit arm.

- I discovered that there was a difference between what my mother paid for things and what she charged for things. It was called "markup," and it was a good thing.

- I learned that I wanted to work for myself and start my own business.

When I look back on my mother's business model, I can see that it was nearly identical to the traditional business model interior designers have been using since the beginning of time. Her expertise and business acumen helped me create a business model that's still in use today by me and many other residential interior designers throughout the country.

A Lesson from Dad

Four months after my family had sunk our savings into Mom's new design studio, my father lost his job through a merger at his company. It never occurred to me that my father wouldn't always work at the same place. It was then that I discovered real loss. No one died; I just found out what it was like not being able to afford the things I wanted at the time.

But there was Norma, my mother, who supported us for eighteen months in a brand-new business. I saw her succeed as an entrepreneur through perseverance and hard work. For her, failure was not an option. She had two boys and a husband to support until he got back on his feet.

She was all we had. As for what I learned from my father's experience: You can't trust a boss with your future!

Can you see how I picked up the entrepreneurial bug? The entrepreneurial gene came from both my mother and my father. A double whammy to be sure, but once I got it, I wasn't foolhardy enough to just dive in headfirst. No, I wanted to gain experience before I took the plunge. I worked for other people and learned how the real world operates before I started my own business.

When I did finally hang my shingle, you guessed it: I used Mom's model. It has served me well, and is basically the same model today as it was nearly thirty years ago. Sure, we keep tweaking how we make money, where we make money, and what gives us income. But once you set up the framework of the model, you really can work within it for the span of a career without changing the essence of the operation. Somewhere out there, I'm certain Mom is smiling.

THE SKINNY ON BUSINESS EDUCATION

You're already getting the hang of this business modeling, aren't you? Well, keep at it. Years down the line, you can thank us for teaching you how to do it right. Frankly, we're impressed to see you pick it up so quickly, considering that most design schools don't offer much of an education when it comes to building a business model or understanding pricing methods.

Want to know a dirty little secret? When it comes to invoicing, collecting, inventory, tear sheets, balance sheets, billing, purchase orders, profits, loss, etc., most designers don't have a clue. The most business advice 75 percent of us get is "Plug into QuickBooks Pro and go." It's a shameful revelation, but so very true. This naturally makes a fundamental business education that much more valuable, so by all means, continue reading.

As for that fancy diploma you have hanging on the wall, would it be that blasphemous for us to say you might want to try getting some of your money back? An eight-week "Business Practices" course (standard for most design schools) is not enough education for the manager of a Pizza Hut, let alone a professional interior designer.

Every designer we've ever met complains about the lack of business education in design schools, yet things never seem to change. Why is there such a disconnect between academia and the design world? Could it be that they have their academic heads stuck in the proverbial sand?

The stigma surrounding design dates back to our humble roots in the home economics department, when decorating was viewed as an avocation—a hobby for housewives rather than a bona fide industry. Feeding the cliché, design schools never seemed to get around to changing the designer's image from the harebrained flibbertigibbet to the business entrepreneur.

That's too bad, because now the industry is a giant box office hit. Many designers are raking in billions annually. Yet, so few designers know how to count. It's great that professors are talking about green designs and all, but even eco-friendly design skills won't buy you a cup of coffee if you can't make a business run properly. Enough said.

UNDERSTANDING PRICING METHODS

Not to put you on the spot, but now let's take some inventory. You have a pretty good idea of your mission, segment, structure, product, and market—so now let's delve further into basic money matters and talk about how you are going to bill your clients. After all, this is called show *business*, not show *friendship*. As a designer, you must decide early on what pricing methods you're going to employ, or you will continue to get paid like you're in the eighth grade.

Many design chiefs take pride in cleverly blending the pricing methods you're about to read about to best suit their design skills and business goals. Once you've gotten the pricing options down, you may decide to give our pricing blend a whirl or experiment with a unique recipe of your own. Remember, there are no wrong answers. Your blend will be what's right for you and your clients. To get you started, your basic pricing options are provided below.

Retail

Retail is by far the most familiar pricing method. Most of us have been charged retail all of our lives. It is the American way, and yet no one really wants to pay retail, do they? Actually, some clients do—especially in the design world, where retail is most popular with hybrid designers who offer their design services out of a retail shop. While some hybrid designers may charge design fees, most make their profits off the sale of furniture and textiles—whatever is in their store—and throw in their design services for free for VIP clients.

This is not exactly the way to get people clamoring for your designs, but it works for a lot of people. Some other uses of retail in the marketplace can be found in the methods of designers who charge clients no retainer or design fee in order to sell them goods at retail. In our humble opinion, this is the least attractive pricing method.

Cost-Plus Markup

Cost-plus markup is the amount a designer adds to the "cost" price of goods in order to cover overhead and profit. Some call it cost-plus percentage, cost plus, percentage plus, or just plain markup. Whatever you deem it, marking up product is a huge profit arm for most design entrepreneurs. It allows designers to make a profit on the goods they sell, not just on their design fees.

Whether one charges a design fee or not, purveyors of the cost-plus markup method mark up every piece of furniture and every yard of fabric they sell to their clients. This is by no means some kind of sneaky maneuver. Rather, reputable designers agree with their clients on a set markup percentage at the beginning of a project.

Considering the issue of markups, the question on everyone's enterprising mind should be, How high is too high? If you ask our friends in the academic world who still don't see interior design as a business, they will say markups should be unrealistically low, with time charges and add-ons making up part of the shortfall.

This may be the way some designers do business, but we don't see the point. If you ask us, millions of dollars are left on the table every year because young designers don't want to break rank with their ASID brethren. We say, Get paid what you are worth.

CASE STUDY: DESIGNER SCHADENFREUDE REARS ITS UGLY HEAD

Recently, at an ASID-sponsored event in our area, a past ASID chapter president and a young designer we know were chatting about business and the subject of design fees came up. When the young designer told this person what she charges per hour ($150) the lady went ballistic: "You're still a student! How could you have the nerve to charge that much money?"

In fact, the fee was set by discussions with us in the office, her student advisor, and the company with whom she had created a strategic alliance. Once she set her rates, within three months, she brought in three separate design clients, who all paid the retainer. The past president at the party even had the nerve to bring up that she sat on an ASID business practices committee, and that they were reviewing their position on how and when fees should be set. What's next—everyone across the United States having to charge the same fee? We always use the old adage, "The proof is in the pudding." In this case, the "pudding" is clients who choose to pay the young designer's fee.

We decided to go online to ascertain the naysayer's business model and the type of business she ran. After all, here she was talking business practices and how they could best be applied to fees. We wanted to give her our two cents. But here's the kicker: Once online, we could not find a single listing for the woman or her design company.

She isn't listed in the yellow pages or the telephone book. What does that tell you? It tells us she's a "paper" designer who talks the talk but doesn't, and obviously can't, walk the walk. How can anyone respect anything she might have to say about how someone else should conduct business? This woman, who is a member of ASID, doesn't even have a Web site, a business number, or any position in the community.

Gadflies such as this have to stop trying to tell us how to do business. Their protectionist position does nothing to promote the business of interior design. As you enter into the professional world, do not listen to unkind and stupid drivel from people who purport to be professionals but couldn't find their way to profitability if they tried. These designers need to be brought to task for their outmoded and monolithic ideas. They are probably not truly reflective of ASID, but maybe that organization should review its position as compared to that of some local members.

THE HALE-WILLIAMS PRICING FORMULA

So, you want to know our dirty trade secrets, do you? You're getting rather personal, but okay—just promise you won't tell anyone. While we mark up product to what is generally referred to as retail, in truth, we use a formula based on how much the product costs us.

Other firms use a set percentage for markup—for example, cost plus 35 percent. But if you break that figure down in real terms, a markup of 35 percent only gives a small return on investment: a profit margin of only 26 percent. And that's before overhead and taxes.

Even if a designer adds hourly charges into the mix, they're still passing up a ton of profit just because some have declared we're not supposed to be retail "shopkeepers." We say, Get over it. There is nothing wrong with charging markup. We all need to make a realistic profit while we work to create the very best interiors for our clients.

Hourly or Per Diem

In addition to cost-plus markup, most designers charge an hourly rate or per diem for their services. Often combined with markup and a retainer or design fee, it's a great way for young designers to get paid for their time. Almost every professional firm will charge for time whether or not they mark up product.

Of course, Hale-Williams charges for time. We mix in an hourly rate of $275 and charge it against a $5,500 retainer for our design services. Once we've worked off the retainer, we charge clients hourly for our services until the project is complete. While other firms prefer to charge higher hourly rates and sell goods at cost (not our favorite type of business model), it's really up to you as to how creative you want to get. Use your imagination and make sure you make a profit. Charge a healthy rate and don't back off it.

Design Retainers

Want to meet a designer's best friend? Design retainers are usually non-refundable deposits given from client to designer in order to secure their services. Most design firms charge some sort of retainer. While other designers charge a nominal retainer fee and then bill each month for time used, Hale-Williams bases our retainer figure on the amount of time we expect the initial preparation for the presentation to take—usually around twenty hours, for a retainer of $5,500.

As for when we go on the clock, or start charging our clients, we usually ask for a retainer after the initial meeting and before the first big client presentation. While the first client meeting is at no charge, a retainer is needed to pay for the design time before the presentation.

Flat Design Fees

A pricing trend we see going around today is the flat design fee. When they say "flat fee," some designers really mean it. Instead of charging a retainer and then billing hours against it, a lot of designers ask for a flat fee, period. We certainly see its benefit for certain projects.

Let's say a designer is offered a small job that may take two to ten hours to complete. If the designer suggests a flat fee based on a healthy estimate, he or she will make a profit whether it takes two hours or ten to complete. It's just a different way to ensure profit. Remember, clients are going to pay the retainer either way. Even young designers can charge a flat design fee. (Heck, so can old ones: We're seriously considering changing our model from cost-plus markup and a retainer to a flat design fee!)

BILLING METHODS

Are your eyes wide open now? If you're new to the business school, we know it's a lot to take in, but once you've digested your latest batch of brain food, we want to examine the way designers apply pricing methods in billing clients. There are two general schools of thought that are predominant in today's marketplace. In their purest forms, they are called the transparent pricing and the presented pricing methods.

The "New School" Method

Transparent pricing is a line-item cost breakdown that discloses to clients the actual price (and markup) for each product included in a residential or commercial project. It is used by New School designers who usually charge clients a professional design fee in addition to a marked-up, or transparent, price for every piece of furniture and yard of fabric procured.

What's interesting about the New School method is that on top of the professional design fee, most make cost-plus markup. What's unfortunate about the New School methodology is that designers cannot charge clients until they themselves have received the bills from their furniture, fabric, or accessory dealers. This means that something we call "transparent billing" can dribble on for weeks after a designer has installed a piece. On far too many occasions, a client will end up paying for a delivery a month after he or she has received a piece of furniture or has had a room wallpapered. For some, this may sound fine, but we personally find it repulsive.

The "Classic" Method

To understand the tremendous impact of the New School on the design industry, let's step back to a time before the New School, professional organizations, or transparent pricing existed. Back in the "old days," there was a palpable air of glamour and mystery around hiring a designer. This was in part because as with buying a Mercedes-Benz automobile, designers presented clients with a single price in bidding on a project. We call this method the stated or delivered price, which refers to the "total cost" for the custom order, delivery, and installation of a piece of art, furniture, window treatment, textile, product, accessory, antique, etc.

For designers and clients, the obvious benefit of the stated price is knowing in advance exactly what an item will cost, including delivery. They know interior designers certainly come with a designer price tag, but as for transparency and getting a line-item breakdown of the cost? Forget about it. Fifty years ago, no client ever dared ask how a designer worked his or her magic. Today, most clients want to know every detail to ensure they are getting the best possible deal.

The Presented Price versus the Flat Fee

Some of you are probably asking what the difference is between a presented price and a flat fee. When designers confuse the two, we suspect they aren't talking about the same thing. When we say "presented price," we don't mean quoting a fee for an entire job. It's how each individual piece is priced. On the other hand, a flat fee is for the complete design of a home or office, inclusive of furnishings, accessories, installations, shipping, etc.

The Benefits of Stated Pricing

Would it surprise you to learn that some practitioners of the stated price method are still operating successfully today? Would it further surprise you to learn that we're two of those proud practitioners? We realize it may sound archaic to some of you greenhorns, but Hale-Williams Interiors has proudly employed stated pricing for all of the many years we've been in business. We love it so much that we consider stated pricing to be one of the foundations of our business philosophy.

We use stated pricing in quoting clients' estimates for custom-made pieces of furniture, draperies, upholstery, art, etc. We've even been known to apply it to some small jobs, single rooms, or entire projects from time to time.

Granted, estimating the total cost for an item, inclusive of custom design, ordering, delivery, and installation, may be more difficult for new designers who are still learning about markup and profit margin. In the end, however, we promise that its application across the board will yield more money. The benefits of stated pricing are that it:

- Allows a better markup and profit margin on goods sold
- Lets you add a little sugar to the deal during negotiations to make the price more appealing to both parties
- Allows younger designers to charge less for their time in the beginning to help build clientele

With all the overhead costs of operating a business today, even with all the designer fees, hourly rates, and cost markups, every job needs additional income to succeed. Are you sold on stated pricing yet? Do you want to know how we sell our pricing model to clients?

The logic goes like this: When buying a Mercedes-Benz automobile, one pays a set price, right? Well, no one asks a Mercedes-Benz dealer how much the brake pedal costs, how much the rearview mirror costs, or how much the transmission costs. So, why should a designer divulge the cost of every yard of fabric used in the installation of a client's window treatment?

Everything we do is custom-made, just as it is for Mercedes-Benz. Every product and service we sell is a luxury, just like a Mercedes-Benz. All of our clients are affluent and can afford what we charge, just like Mercedes-Benz's clients. And just like Mercedes-Benz, we do a superior job. If you want a discount ride, go buy a Volkswagen.

Personal philosophy aside, young designers must decide on a pricing model that best fits their style. Never base pricing strategies on what everyone else is doing. What it boils down to is this: With transparent pricing, there is simply no incentive for the designer to find a better price for a client. When a client knows the base cost and set markup fee, there is no room for negotiation.

Actual Costs for Completing a Sale

New School pricing also doesn't take into account the actual costs of completing the sale. With transparent pricing, there is a markup of a percentage called the gross, or before-cost, profit. From the gross, one must remove the cost of each and every hand that touches the sale. This means the cost for people who:

- Write the purchase order
- Fax, e-mail, or mail the order
- Pay for e-mail, fax, and phone service and buy the stamps
- Follow up on orders to ensure receipt
- Receive the delivered goods
- Review the order once received
- Produce invoices
- Handle accounts for payroll, etc.

Add it up; it's an expensive process! Sure, many firms charge hourly for this type of administrative work, but does that charge really cover the actual costs? In the end, there isn't any "net" profit on this type of sale. With our pricing model, we know we are achieving around a 10- to 12-percent net margin of profit. To us, that is a good return on investment.

AN INDUSTRY DIVIDED

Want another history lesson? After professional design organizations like ASID began suggesting that their members adopt the transparent pricing method, many in the design community predictably began looking down their upturned noses at those in the profession who, they were sure, were doing business absolutely, positively, and completely "the wrong way."

As with any good turf war, many independent designers promptly started choosing sides: In one corner were the uptown, stated price designers, and in the other were the trendy, downtown, transparent price designers. Which side should a young, hot designer on the rise choose? Like we said, it isn't about declaring allegiance or choosing sides. If a designer can sell his or her pricing method to clients, he or she doesn't have to be loyal to either school.

We truly believe that you, as a modern designer, have the freedom to mix these two pricing philosophies to find the perfect blend that best suits your individual business model. That said, factors like clientele, sales skills, reputation, and experience will largely determine what philosophy you eventually decide to adopt.

As you know, when it comes to pricing, the old adage, " You can't teach an old dog new tricks," still rings true for Hale-Williams Interior Design. This is especially true because the "new trick" is significantly less rewarding than the old one! Who can really blame some of us "old dogs" for resisting change? No professional designer in his or her right mind would abandon a successful business model for one that isn't nearly as lucrative. Our uptown clientele, some of whom have been working with us for years, weren't crying for reform. They were, and still are, happily on board with our pricing model. So, how is this industry divide even an established designer's problem?

That's simple: The great industry divide is every designer's problem, regardless of your age, your reputation, or what "side" you're on. When our industry is branded as inconsistent, unethical, and unorganized, everyone's bottom line is affected. No amount of public relations can overcome a growing negative perception among clients.

When it comes to pricing, we try to educate our clients at each phase of a project. First, we ask them to give us their overall budget for a particular room or an entire house. We like to break it down per room because we realize most clients don't want to spend as much on the guest bedroom as they do on the master bedroom, kitchen, or living room.

After clients give us their budget, we examine it before providing a realistic budget for what we can do for them, based on:

- The scope of the project
- What the client wants
- What we, as designers, see we can do to realize the vision
- The things and the images they have shown us

We don't break down the price by design fee or what it's going to cost for each yard of fabric. We offer a stated price and monitor it. Sometimes we go over the budget, and sometimes we go under it.

Most of the time, the budget variance has a lot to do with clients choosing the more expensive table over a less expensive alternative when the more expensive piece fits better or will take their room to another level. But the client makes the decision; it's up to them to keep the budget in line or not. We are merely at their service.

DON'T PANIC AND LOWER RATES

Whatever you do, don't lower your fees to get your foot in the door. Instead, take on smaller projects in which you only have to work a few hours. That way, you can charge a smaller design fee and you won't have to compromise your pricing philosophy.

Some designers inevitably will disagree with this strategy. They will tell you to take every job in the beginning and find a way to make it work. We think that's a mistake. You can't stay in business for long if you're cutting your rates at every sign of trouble. If you are really having trouble landing clients, don't blame your price tag: This is the time to reevaluate how you do business.

Think about how you can refine your business model so that you have more opportunities to make money. One solution is to create more profit arms.

We know a design team in Florida who were completely focused on the specialized world of country club design. They were doing great and had even expanded their practice until a year ago, when their business bottomed out. When nothing was happening on the country club scene, what did they do?

First, they e-mailed their network of design colleagues to let them know they were interested in partnering on projects. Then, they went back to their list of potential clients and let everyone know that their firm was now taking on smaller projects and doing renovation work.

With a little business-model brainstorming, our friends in the Sunshine State evolved their business. Now they don't have to rely on one specialty profit stream (i.e., country clubs). They do renovations and upholstery work. Soon after they made the change, they were commissioned to reupholster one thousand chairs by a country club that had not hired them for a complete remodel in the past. Because the partners evolved their business model, new business came their way.

For young designers, don't be afraid to mix and match pricing models. Try using a stated price for most goods, but charging a flat percentage markup fee for antiques, rugs, and art. Whether you use hybrid pricing or a straight stated price, if you're able to avoid 100-percent transparency by selling your "unique" pricing philosophy to prospective clients, you just may be able to ensure an annual profit margin for your business that keeps you growing, in the black, and ready to design for another day.

THE PRICING "TRIPLE CROWN"

There are three steps to the "triple crown" of pricing. Step one is having an in-house formula. Every design firm should have a formula for charging clients that is created in-house and applies across the board. Your formula for marking up or charging fees should apply to *all* clients, or there will be trouble.

The second step in triple-crown pricing looking toward your clouds of income. Once you "get out there," you're going to notice that there are certain areas of the design business that are more lucrative than others. If you are looking to improve business, identify the areas from which you profit and eliminate the rest. If you make more marking up antiques but can't seem to break even selling art, guess which one you should cut from your agenda?

Step three is employing the one-percent rule. One of the worst mistakes you can make is undervaluing your services. It is crucial that you understand the market and your worth in it. Don't be afraid to raise your rates a little bit. One percent is huge. We know some designers who think that if they raise their fees, everyone is going to notice. Generally, your clients never notice. We are the only ones who are so afraid. Once you start bumping up rates, keep raising them a little bit annually. Remember, don't raise your fees $50 an hour; raise them $10 an hour. Every added percent goes to the bottom line.

CHAPTER 7

MARKETING YOUR BUSINESS

*Networking, Public Relations,
and Advertising*

"To have great poets, there must be
great audiences, too."

—WALT WHITMAN

How are your entrepreneurial spirits now, my young upstarts? Be honest. Are you invigorated? Intimidated? Or are you 100 percent sure you aren't sure? For those of you wondering if those "mixed feelings" you're having amount to designer blasphemy, the answer is: Absolutely not. Behind the swaggers of most budding entrepreneurs are wardrobes full of self-doubt. That is truly living the entrepreneurial question.

We'll say it again: Don't equivocate yourself into inaction. In this business, stasis spells death, so come to grips with your entrepreneurial fears and desires as early as possible, or you may miss your window of opportunity by sitting on the fence. If you ask a couple of ambitious guys like us, "not answering your calling" has to be one of the worst lots in life.

Think about it: Could you really live with being one of those people who claim to have pursued their dreams and failed, but in reality never even tried? We couldn't, and we don't think you could, either.

MARKETING: THE BIG PICTURE

Though fear of failure can be a great motivator, let's switch gears from a discussion of all of the roadblock "what ifs" to a conversation that courageously asks, "What now?" Seeing as you are all grown-up designers, it's high time we stopped treading in uncertain waters and took off those training wheels. Here is what we will assume from now until the end of the book:

- You are a talented designer.
- You are learning to be a savvy businessperson.
- You will start your own design business.

Now, let's get into how a budding entrepreneur goes about building a solid foundation for his or her business. Need we remind you that even in building the tallest skyscraper, one must start construction at ground level?

Marketing Makes the World Go 'Round

Hypothetically speaking, if you were to randomly select ten successful design businesses and study their blueprints, you'd be amazed at how diverse their business models, clientele, methods of operation, and design products and services were. As for the common thread, other than the fact that they are all successful design companies, one parallel would almost certainly be each company's savvy use of marketing—in all its modern forms—to sell their wares to the public.

Call it marketing, publicity, or exposure, but do your career a favor and understand the crucial role this force must play in the prosperity of your design firm, or prepare to get burned right out of the chute. Whether it's great marketing, publicity, advertising, networking, public relations, positioning, or branding, you'd better believe that all successful businesses depend on it to flourish.

Young design entrepreneurs should be able to nimbly employ the nuances of marketing even before they start thinking about pouring the foundation of their own design firm. Think about it in real terms: If you don't know how to market your business properly, how on earth is anyone going to show up for your grand opening? They probably won't.

Are Your Ducks in a Row?

Here are some essential questions every entrepreneur must answer before beginning to market a business:

- Do you have a business model?
- Do you have a marketing plan?
- Have you done the research to know your market?
- Have you done the research to know your clients?
- Do you know what kind of work you are looking for?
- Do you know the capabilities of your own firm?
- Do you know your firm's goals?

If you answered a resounding "nay" to all of the above, don't worry. We will gently guide you through the process so that you will be ready for anything. The first step is learning what great marketing can do for you and your future business.

Some of our country's founding fathers would probably choke on their populist ideals to learn that in America today, great marketing has become just as important as (if not more important than) developing a great product or outstanding service. (You mean talent, hard work, and a great product aren't all there is to success? If only it were so, my naïve apprentice; if only it were so.)

Here in the real world, great marketing is one of the most powerful, intangible factors in the free marketplace. When deftly executed, it can earn a design entrepreneur riches, fame, and glory. Of course, the flipside is that bad marketing will quickly sink your entrepreneurial ship.

What Is Marketing?

You've now determined that good marketing is something you absolutely can't live without. But what is marketing, anyway? Marketing is:

- How designers communicate
- The way designers present themselves to the design community, be it to prospective clients, media members, or other "players" in the design world
- How designers get their business "out there" in front of potential clients

Sounds easy, right? For some of you outgoing types, it will be, while for others, not exactly. Though many designers are natural self-promoters, marketing a business can be a tricky game. Surviving on instinct alone rarely cuts the mustard.

Every neophyte designer should take a few seminars or college courses to learn more about the differences among marketing, positioning, and advertising as they relate to interior design. Each really is a different discipline that requires a slightly different point of view.

THE ELEVATOR SPEECH

One of the first marketing tools you must master is your elevator speech. It describes what your business does within fifteen to twenty seconds, and uses no more than approximately fifty words. The elevator speech is your most fundamental verbal weapon in attracting clients. Your message must be concise, to the point, and just a little about "blowing your own horn."

Try writing out a few ideas, then speak them aloud, preferably in front of a mirror. It may sound silly, but once you're comfortable with the tone and length, try it out on a few of your friends. Avoid memorizing this speech. Instead, try to get the same sort of patter each time you open your mouth to talk shop. Once you have your patter down pat, the ultimate test, as you know, is to give it a whirl at a business meeting or a cocktail party.

It goes without saying that your speech needs to express that you are not only a talented designer but also an honest, trustworthy businessperson. But here's the tricky part: You must also paint your professional story with a compelling personal touch that's not too personal. Let us explain.

A Verbal Snapshot

This exercise is sometimes hard for new designers, because they may not believe their lives are all that interesting or exciting. We contend, however, that *all* of us, young or old, have interesting facets to ourselves that don't necessarily reveal too much about our personal lives but allow clients to feel as if they've gotten just a little closer to us as human beings.

Personal touches can be anything from talking about sailing, camping, or cooking to reading or whatever the designer can dream up. So think about what you want to convey in your speech as far as your services, style, and business model are concerned, then weave in your personal touch.

In crafting your speech, remember that you will soon be selling the services of a business instead of the services of an individual designer. Get used to speaking for an entity that is removed from you personally. When you are operating a business, most clients will want to know less about the principal designer's hobbies and more about the makeup of your personnel, how your billings are achieved, and how professional your firm is in terms of operational procedures and providing great customer service.

Elevator Evolution

Enough talking; let's show you an example of how one of our elevator speeches has evolved over the years.

When I (Tom) was a young designer, my first elevator speech was: "My name is Tom Williams and I own and operate T. Lawton Williams Interior Design." Not exactly awe-inspiring, is it? Well, I was young (so give me a break!), but as I grew older and more confident, I started adding a few things here and there, such as the type of design I do and the other types of services I offer.

One thing I learned early on was to make my elevator speech snappy. It can't last forever. If it does, some people will lose interest, while others will just think you're exceptionally boastful and talkative. So, start working on a snappy version of your speech, and be patient. It takes time to come up with the perfect pitch, tone, and delivery.

After a lifetime of practice, I think I've finally come up with my great elevator speech. Want to hear it? It's short and sweet, and it goes like this: "My name is Tom Williams of Hale-Williams Interior Design, an award-winning luxury residential interior design and project management firm located in Carmel, California."

Rolls off the tongue like butter, doesn't it? Not really? Well, it works for me, and that really is the point. Create your own elevator speech that works for you and your clients, then unleash it on the world.

24/7 MARKETING

As you know, aspiring entrepreneurs should begin marketing themselves "24/7" before starting a business. But what does "24/7 marketing" mean, exactly? It means talking about your design skills to anyone who will listen, getting invited to speak as a professional designer whenever possible, and always showing up on time and prepared. You never know who could be watching or listening.

Almost any social situation can be turned into a marketing windfall for your business if you know the message you want to convey and know how to make it part of the conversation without coming across as pushy or high-handed.

For all you skeptics, here is a real-world example of how 24/7 marketing can turn a casual social event into a business bonanza for your design firm. Our story begins just after we moved to Baltimore and knew no one in town. Somehow, we were invited to attend a champagne tasting at a local bar. We thought, Why not? We like champagne—let's go. But we really had no expectations going in.

We gathered at the appointed site in a room above the bar and met the owner, his father, and one of his cousins. Once we sat down, we struck up conversations with a few of the couples seated nearby. Little did we know that six months later the couple seated to our right was going to hire us to design their Baltimore home and then hire us to design their vacation home on the eastern shore of the Chesapeake Bay.

If you think we scored big time, consider that we also became so friendly with the owners of the bar, they eventually hired us to renovate the room in which we had the tasting. Voila! A designer hat trick! All three projects came from relationships we fostered by utilizing 24/7 marketing at a random social event. Not a bad payoff, if we do say so ourselves.

Marketing Tip Sheet

Here are a few more 24/7 marketing tips to keep you busy while you work on developing a blueprint for your business.

- Give talks to professional or design-related clubs
- Join professional, social, and networking groups
- Create your own seminars and design events
- Join and participate in professional design organizations
- Participate in designer show houses to increase visibility
- Write design-related articles for anyone who will print your work
- Target projects that will generate editorial press
- Have your work photographed in newspapers and regional magazines
- Look for every opportunity to "strut your stuff" on television

The whole idea with marketing is to increase your exposure by strategically putting yourself out there. That means you're going to have to get used to always being "on" when you venture out in public.

Develop a Professional Persona

Try talking to a group of professional designers, and you'll find that most of them believe it's important to have an "on" switch. You should start developing yours now. It may sound corny to prepare to such a degree, but preparation works, particularly for designers who aren't naturally gregarious or outgoing. For those designers to be effective, they need to gear up to be poised and on point.

Whether you're a naturally gregarious social butterfly or a "butterfly in-training," get out there and flap your stylish wings. Remember, you are the embodiment of your future business. All eyes just may be on you. So, try not to trip over anything.

Now that you've outgrown your school clothes, it's time to think about graduating to a business suit. When a designer dons his or her professional persona, it's like putting on an enhanced version of him or herself for everyone else to see. That's not to say your public persona isn't really you, because it is; it's just a magnified version of your best qualities that you need to help your business shine on the professional stage.

Think of it like putting on your best Sunday suit. If you are aware of the difference between you and your public designer persona, it makes it easier to switch gears into designer mode. All of us have our professional suits, so don't be ashamed to hone yours, press it, and make it the best it can be.

Sharpen Your People Skills

But what if you are a shy darling? The longer we live, the more we hear that even shy adults are able to learn how to be more open and outgoing. For many designers, developing a public image is less a god-given talent than an acquired skill. We know because as boys and as young men, we were very shy.

Once we realized our shyness wasn't going to work in our chosen profession, we made an effort to read about how to meet people. We enrolled in speech classes and put ourselves in situations where we had to walk up to people and introduce ourselves. Although we had not yet met, by the time we were in our respective colleges, we had mastered some of the basic skills needed to succeed in marketing. After you get over the proverbial hump, public speaking isn't as daunting as it appears from the back row. In fact, you may be surprised to find you actually begin to like it.

Putting Your Marketing Skills to Work

When we started in this business, we weren't social butterflies. In fact, we didn't have a clue about marketing ourselves. It was only after we had worked for other people that we began to see how effective marketing really worked. By continuing our real-world education through seminars and networking with other designers, we quickly learned how marketing could help our business.

By the time we finally went into business for ourselves, we were ready to go 24/7. We looked for marketing opportunities at every turn. We appeared at schools, churches, meetings, clubs, and just about anywhere that would have us. Go ahead—give it a whirl and see if you can follow suit in your own fabulous way. Have no fear.

SIZING UP YOUR TARGET MARKET

So, you're working on your marketing plan and your public persona, and you have your elevator speech down pat. To whom are you going to pitch it? In other words, who are your clients? If, while thumbing through your empty Rolodex, you realize you don't have any clients, riddle us this: Who would you like your clients to be? Think about it. This is what we call understanding your target market.

Your target market is generally a result of your business plan. For example, if you were going into commercial design, your target market would be businesses and corporations. If you were diving into residential, your target market would be homeowners living in your part of the world.

In order to clearly see the market that's for you, it's time to dust off your reading glasses and do some market research. Did you really think you were going to skate through our course without hitting the books? Not on our watch.

While it's true that client referrals will always be the "bread and but-ter" of established design firms, you aren't established yet; you need clients right now. Look around and see who might like your ideas and design phi-losophy. Where do these people buy design services? How often do they buy design services, and how much do they pay for those services?

Market Research Tips

Here are some more questions to ask yourself while you size up your target market:

- How many designers are in your area?
- What are their specialties?
- How old is your target market?
- Where does your target market live?
- How much do they earn?
- How do they spend their money?
- Are there new housing developments in the area?
- How is the home renovation market?
- Can you afford the rent and staff?
- Is there a constant influx of new residents?

You can learn so much from studying your clients and the industry through the eyes of the media. Once you've figured out your target audi-ence, start reading what they read, like design magazines and the social pages. Go where your clients go, see what they are into, and then build your services around what appeals to them most.

Absorb as much information as possible. Study how typical consumers spend money. Drill down and get to know who these clients are and where they live, work, and play. Let's say you are targeting the twenty-five- to thirty-five-year-old demographic. Define how people in this age group spend their time and, especially, their money. We guarantee you'll uncover valuable information that will help you attract your type of client.

What Type of Client Should You Seek?

Would all you aspiring big-time designers like some insider information? As a rule of thumb, the "higher end" the market you are trying to attain, the older, for the most part, your clientele is going to be. Studies show that younger clients typically spend most of their income on housing, furnishings (the essentials), children, schooling, and savings. That means most clients under forty do not have the disposable income to hire a high-end designer.

Are you beginning to see why we suggest targeting older clients if you want to make big bucks in residential? We've found it really isn't until about the age of forty when clients begin to have the extra money to employ designers. In our opinion, this factor alone makes the "forty and older" pond the most appealing demographic, as it's the one stocked with the highest number of ideally qualified clients.

Don't take our word for it—get out there and do the work! Find out what market is best for you, and once you've determined which clients are worth your time, think about what is realistic for your business. Ask yourself tough questions like, Do I really have the resources and connections to go after elite clients?

It goes without saying that larger commissions get the most mindshare once they are secured, but how much time should be spent securing these clients rather than feeding the family on smaller commissions be? It's a tough call, but keep in mind that a lot of designers are going after the elite clients. Sometimes, the most profitable projects come from smaller clients.

It's true: Smaller fish can be tasty morsels, especially in the early part of your career. Some small clients have even been known to appreciate the one-on-one attention of a charming young designer so much that they open up their wallets and hire the designer for other projects or make referrals to friends. The choice is yours. In the end, your job is to make a great, lasting impression no matter whom you are working for or what you are doing.

Study Your Competition

Let's downshift our focus from potential clients to your heated competition. Panning the landscape, the first thing you will notice is that competition for every client is fierce, so let's simplify things by breaking your adversaries down into two categories: the pretenders and the contenders.

The pretenders are the scores of unqualified "paper" designers you see littering the modern arena. You've no doubt met them before. They are not so hot: Their work is middling and their marketing skills are weak, but all too often, these designers can become thorns in your side as they find ways to underbid professional designers (who naturally charge more).

Find out who these pretenders are and study their moves. You'll find they're often modern "ladies with taste" or well-funded "paper" decorette designers who have little to no formal design training. How do they operate? Usually by promising the moon, charging less, and then not delivering. Professionally, these designers are blights on the industry; personally, they are a threat to you because they take food off your plate. Get to the point where you can smell one coming from a mile away, then avoid them like the plague.

As for your professional counterparts, don't be afraid to make the first move by introducing yourself, particularly with designers you admire. You don't want to stalk them, but your goal should be to foster relationships with designers who may be able to mentor you. As you know from earlier chapters, we feel it's a great idea to align yourself with other successful designers, so don't be afraid to work with the ones you trust.

Study the Finest

While you do market research, do take some time to expose yourself to what the elite clients are buying. Get out and sample the high-end products and see what they are like. What if it's out of your price range? Who cares? You still need to know what's "the best" in order to ascertain value for your clients.

We aren't saying that all designers should go into the luxury design game; it's just that high-end shopping is fun as well as beneficial for any neophyte's career. For one thing, it allows you to spot shoddily made rip-offs and clearly see when something is well made or not. In addition, as you gain design experience, you're going to discover that most of your clients, regardless of how much money they have, will ask you to mix and match luxury pieces with middle-of-the-road pieces in order to stretch their budget. So go on and get a luxury education, breathe in the rarefied air, and have fun. Just leave your credit cards at home.

MARKETING: THE HOLY TRINITY

Now that you're fully steeped in information from your market research, let's go over how you can apply that knowledge to your marketing efforts. As you may or may not know, marketing is divided into three major areas: networking, public relations, and advertising.

Networking

In the design game, it doesn't matter what you know, but who you know and how skillful you are in leveraging your connections to gain exposure and grow your business. Networking is the process of utilizing your circle of industry friends, colleagues, and mentors for your own sake and your clients' sakes.

For all you designer Darwinists, welcome to the real world, where it's every man and woman for him- or herself. May the best networking butterflies win. We hope you take to networking like naturals, because keeping your ear to the designer grapevine is a great way to get that informal postgraduate training we keep telling you about.

Let's be real. You aren't going to learn the things you need to learn in school, and you won't learn many trade secrets from your clients. The truth is, you're probably going to gain the most valuable insights from your network of friends. Having a good network is like having your own designer resource team that helps you toward established designer freedom. So use them or lose them.

In our own narcissistic way, don't we all love to be the first to tell a friend about a hot new restaurant, movie, or play? The same applies to professional referrals. In a world full of self-proclaimed tastemakers, it is important that you meet the right people who, if you tell them your story the right way, will pass your name on to the next person, who will then pass your name on to the next person... and so on. That's how it works in the networking game. When it's done to perfection, good networking buzz can go a long way toward making your career.

So, get out there and mingle, meet, and sidle up to anyone who may be of help, like other designers, realtors, magazine publishers, sales representatives, or specialty craftsmen. Any person who will share your story with potential clients is fair game.

Here are a few networking tips to keep you hot-wired and in the game:

- Stay in touch—Make frequent contact with your design network.

- Stay current—Study the zeitgeist; know what's going on.

- Stay visible—Frequent professional events and networking functions.

- Be bold—Make introductions, be aggressive, and don't be shy.

- Be considerate—Treat your contacts like friends. Get "human" with them. That means send thank-you cards, acknowledge birthdays, attend parties, and always tell them how fabulous they look when you see them.

- Continue your education—Seek out mentors, and don't be shy about asking for help and advice.

- Grow your network—The more connected you are, the better your business will be.

- Join groups—Build your network by joining groups.

- Keep your friends close—If you scratch their back, they'll scratch yours.

- Keep your enemies closer—Befriend your competition. Trust us—it works.

As for Hale-Williams, we use networking daily by working with service groups like the chamber of commerce or rotary club. You may think you are too young for this sort of thing, but you are never too young. It would benefit any designer to take a board position in which he or she can meet other people who are also out in the working world. If the rotary club isn't your thing, try getting on the board of your local art museum or with a charitable organization. Your canvas is empty, so start painting.

Now that you're beginning to see how marketing works, there is, of course, a downside to all this flitting around. You're going to find that, while some networking relationships may turn out to be absolute goldmines, others are going to turn out to be hopeless pits of fool's gold. This is all a part of the risk.

To differentiate between the two, you must stay alert and sober. You have to think clearly to see the world for what it is. Remember, networking time is time on the clock, so make sure you are spending less time socializing and trying to live like your clients (a cardinal sin) and more time cultivating business and adding to your game. If there is no payoff, cut your losses and move on to the next networking pool.

Public Relations

Okay, so you're a networking natural—that's fantastic. You shouldn't mind if we step it up a notch. Public relations is the second tier of marketing, in which an individual or business strategically exposes its services to the public in order to create positive buzz, or word of mouth, in the marketplace.

For us, much of our energy has been directed toward the public relations and marketing side of our business. We have truly spent a lifetime being out there, being seen, doing things, and going places, all of which sounds like one big party, but it's not about the party. It's about the necessity of people seeing you in the public eye.

For whatever reason, a lot of clients like to hire designers who are visible in the public eye. They think that designers with a certain amount of fame or a recognizable brand name must be more talented than the other schlubs they've never heard of. This is America, after all, where perception and image are everything.

If you want to learn more about how to build an outstanding PR messaging platform for your business, there are plenty of public relations courses out there that you can take. We're simply interested in getting you started down the right path. While you process all of this new information, here is how to become a public relations guru in ten easy steps:

- Be a great designer
- Give great client service

- Build a story for your business
- Be a shameless self-promoter
- Be charming
- Do business lunches
- Call on former, current, and prospective clients
- Attend professional and social networking events
- Take pride in your poise and your appearance
- Join organizations, attend conferences, and do charity work

We know what some of you wise guys are thinking: Does every designer have to be in business twenty-five years in order to build solid word of mouth? Aren't there any shortcuts to success? Oh, if only there were shortcuts in life. Then we'd all be rich.

We can't say we know of any shortcuts, but one way to create fairly instant word of mouth is to be fabulously visible. Young designers have been known to generate good buzz by hosting client parties, staying active in the community, garnering press, or executing creative marketing campaigns. But to remain buzz-worthy, a young designer has to have the inner fire (i.e., the motivation) to continue creating good buzz over a long period of time. For all you shortcut artists, the truth is that you've got to want to be in it for the long haul.

Advertising

Unless you're living under a large rock, every aspect of your life is drenched in advertisements. This may sound like an excerpt from an Orwellian nightmare, but in America, we can't escape ads. They are everywhere. Though we're all desensitized to their ever-presence, advertising still has quite a bit of power and influence over the modern consumer. Your mission is to harness that power for the benefit of your firm.

If you haven't heard, effective advertising is the repetitive delivery of a consistent message involving a product people want. Sounds like a mouthful, but in a world full of self-promoters, you'd better be able to talk fast.

Everyone today self-promotes, from the Dalai Lama to the ten-year-old professional skateboarder living down the street, so it goes without saying that every designer must advertise to get anywhere. In the eyes of Jack and Jill Consumer, you're nobody without advertising.

Can you believe it was once considered unprofessional for interior designers to advertise? This taboo dates back to the "ladies with taste" days, when people were designers because they loved design and didn't need the money. Well, in the twenty-first century, that stigma is long gone. Today, everyone needs to advertise, because everyone needs the money.

Good advertising gives the world the image that your firm is prosperous and on the rise. It's a great way to plug your business because of the potential to reach a large audience. The goal is for people to be aware of your firm beyond the fact that it merely exists, so try to be creatively concise in building a compelling story for your ad campaign.

One of the most common things we hear designers say when they aren't busy is, "We need to advertise." Our response is that they should have been doing it all along, especially when they were busy, to keep the momentum rolling.

One of advertising's drawbacks is that it's still not an exact science. Essentially, it's a scatter shooting of exposure, as opposed to marketing and public relations, where you pretty much know your audience. Although the "blanket approach" can work for some national designers, it's a good idea to customize your ad campaigns to appeal to a specific clientele in your part of the country.

If you've done your market research, you should know where to advertise. You know what publications your clients read and where they spend their free time. We highly suggest you advertise locally, instead of nationally, so you can customize your message for a select audience by placing ads on local television stations or in regional or local publications.

Also, don't forget about all the more obvious sources of advertising, like being listed in the yellow pages and on the Internet. To get the most "bang for your buck," you can also hire a media buyer and advertising agency to build and place your ads. If you ask us, however, it's more cost-effective to develop and place them yourself.

If you're one of the many "busy" designers who say they barely have time to read this book, much less take an advertising seminar, we say: find the time. While you are busy rearranging your schedule for the betterment of your career, here are some creative advertising tips for the twenty-first century design entrepreneur to get you through the day.

Our first tip is to start a blog. Right now, there just aren't enough interior design–specific blogs out there. There should be more. For the technologically challenged, a blog (Weblog) is a Web site on which an individual or group of users produces an ongoing narrative. Once you've built your Web site, it is a simple matter to start a blog.

Though blogging will require a time commitment to create regular entries, it's a great way to create free "buzz" for your business and draw traffic to your Web site. Give it a shot. Once you start cross-referencing other blogs (and they do yours), it's amazing what can happen. It's like virtual networking. As a matter of fact, this very book is a result of the blog I (Tom) created in September of 2007. Tad Crawford, publisher at Allworth Press, was looking for someone interested in writing a book on the business of interior design. In late June of 2008, he went to Google and typed in "the business of interior design." As it turns out, my blog was the second to appear in the list, and Tad took a look. As they say, the rest is history. Tad contacted me and asked if I was interested in writing a book. What he didn't know was that we had already written the book and were looking for a publisher. The product of this serendipity is the book you now hold in your hand—one result of a successful overall digital marketing program.

Our second tip is to garner press. Whether it's in newspapers, in magazines, or on television, managing to gain some press in the early part of one's career is invaluable free advertising. Everyone really should try for this exposure, as visual coverage in print or on TV will go a long way toward creating your brand recognition.

For us, appearing on TV fairly early in our careers in Baltimore was a huge step. We were fearless about what we were going to say and do, and simply went on TV and talked about our business. For some reason we really weren't frightened. We had nerves, yes, but they were along the lines of mild stage fright—nothing more. We hope you are just as comfortable.

For some of you, putting yourselves out there for public scrutiny may sound painful, but trust us—it will bring many more returns than just sitting in your office and waiting for the phone to ring.

Can you tell we think the marketing angle of the design game is a huge deal? Well, we do—and it is—but we aren't so caught up in hoopla as to suggest that young designers target projects with the sole intent of generating press. All the media in the world won't amount to much if your work isn't top-notch.

Don't get ahead of yourself while you're "cutting your teeth." Try focusing less on making the cover of *Architectural Digest* and more on having sound business practices, getting established, and becoming a professional design entrepreneur. Sure, large luxury projects will definitely attract attention, but so will unique smaller projects. While you do good work, stay dialed in to what's hot in the design world and begin to look for ways to "frame" one of your projects for the media. That brings us to tip number three: frame your own quality experience.

Tip number four is that every story has an angle. Look at what sells today. Does your work have any interesting angles that might play well in print or on television? Have you just finished a project for a really cool older couple in a new retirement community or recently remodeled a trendy high-rise apartment? Is one of your projects located in the hottest new marina development in town?

If you want another example of a design angle, consider the media's present fascination with designers who can design homes on a do-it-your-self (DIY) budget. Any interesting, small project coming from any of you reading this book could be framed as a "DIY on a Dime" story for televi-sion or print. Other sure fire attention-getters nowadays are projects that illustrate a wonderful use of color or use green designs or products.

Start fleshing out story angles and, if you're having a hard time, keep thinking and be creative. You will find that if you try hard enough, almost every project has a good story angle to garner attention from some audi-ence, somewhere.

Our fifth tip is to pitch an angle. If you are bound and determined to get on television, we suggest you start locally. Try contacting the program manager of a local TV station. These managers are usually young and looking for new talent. They may listen to another young person looking to be seen and heard. Be sure you have a clear idea of what you want to pitch before you start making contact with producers or editors.

Write down your concepts, like, "I want to talk about window treat-ments, upholstery, or lighting." Then, work on pitching your concepts as you did for your elevator speech. Choose a catchy angle that will arouse interest. A great first impression is critical, so go in prepared to work your magic.

Tip six: get a good photographer. If you think you and your work would look great in print, try taking snapshots of your designs and sending them to magazines along with a press release. A media kit will help any media outlet to better see what you've done. It will also make it easier for the programmer or editor to fit you into their schedule.

Speaking of snapshots, hasn't anyone ever told you that a great pho-tographer will get you everywhere in this industry? It's true, but what kind of photographer is right for you? It all depends on your budget and your style. Naturally, the better the photographer you hire, the better your work is going to look.

Since every designer should keep a visual record of all of his or her projects, we suggest you develop a convenient alliance with a great pho-tographer. If he or she is talented and young, it just may be a match made in heaven. The idea is for your photographer to grow his or her business in tandem with yours, photographing your projects as well as (perhaps) your business events.

Just make sure your photographer shoots your projects immediately after completion. Too many designers have found that if you wait too long, your project may look different after the client has had the chance to live in (translation: mess up) your sublime vision.

Our seventh tip is to participate in a showcase home. This participation is an expensive form of advertising that's for designers interested in glamorously strutting their stuff in front of an elite, in-crowd audience. Young luxury residential designers with the appropriate means should definitely consider participating in one simply to build their reputations, make connections, and get exposure.

Just be ready to make a big financial commitment, or find sponsors who will help foot the bill by contributing to your room. Sponsors can be found within your designer network. Ask around; you may convince a furniture or textile maker to sponsor you, or a retail shop owner to donate pieces for display in your showroom. Once again, your success is going to boil down to how well you can sell your story to potential sponsors in the design community.

And our final tip, if you haven't already done so, is to launch a Web site. Every designer must have a great Web site; it is your virtual "shingle" on the World Wide Web. Hale-Williams was in practice for more than fifteen years before the opportunity came along for us to launch a Web site. We've been surfing ever since.

CASE STUDY: THE IMPORTANCE OF A WEB SITE

Tanya Shively, ASID, of Sesshu Design Associates, Ltd., is a member of the Best Practices Network and someone with whom we've worked since 2004. Tanya has an interior design business in Scottsdale, Arizona, and a passion for ecologically responsive design. Her blog (*www. EcoInnovativeDesign.blogspot.com*), is a must-read for anyone creating ecologically sensitive environments. The Sesshu Design Associates, Ltd., Web site incorporates the best tenets of site design, and we asked Tanya to give us a little advice on the subject. Take it away, Tanya!

Valuable Information

Establishing a strong Web presence is a must for every business that wants to be successful. Clients expect to be able to learn more about you, what you do, where you are, etc. by visiting your Web site before they make the decision to contact you. They can also refer others to your work by giving them your Web site's URL. However, an effective Web site really should be more than just an online brochure. In the world of Web 2.0, your Web site functions as an interactive tool for clients to communicate with you, and info is rapidly shared all over the world via e-mail, blogs, and networking sites. This makes having a good site with relevant content and valuable information all the more critical. However, it is also important to remember that not everyone has high-speed Internet, so you want a site to load quickly and easily without needing additional software. Don't let your Web designer talk you into fancy flash pages that are overly large and slow-loading.

Finding the Right Designer

Finding a Web designer who is in sync with your goals and style is important for getting the results that accurately reflect your business. I met with several designers referred by friends and colleagues before finding the Web design team that felt like a good match for my goals. They emphasized their experience in using meta tags and keywords for good search engine optimization, and had designed Web sites for other design-related fields. Being sure that my Web site would be found and ranked favorably by Internet search engines was a key issue. I wanted to be able to make updates and changes to the content easily, without paying someone to make those changes, so they also gave me that capability. Another benefit they offered was that they host Web sites on their own servers, which helps to ensure that the sites don't crash, as can happen with inexpensive domain hosting sites. They are now my one point of contact for any issues relating to my Web site. They provide e-mail and Web mail services as well.

If You Build It, Will They Come?

I started by researching other Web sites and making notes of what I wanted and didn't want before even hiring a designer. Being prepared helped me articulate what I was looking for at the beginning so they didn't waste time coming up with concepts that were not in keeping with my vision. Initially, I showed them a few Web pages that I felt had aspects of what I wanted in my own site, and also some that I didn't like. Providing them with feedback and input at every stage of the process was important, because I knew how I wanted my site to look, function, and feel when completed. I worked for two or three months with the Web designer to tweak and groom the basic layout of the site until it felt right to me.

Understanding your ideal clients is a big key to building a successful site. Taking the time to identify their wants and needs ensures that the money spent in developing and launching your site is not wasted. The second key is creating good copy to make those essential points. Pretty pictures and cool graphics won't mean anything if the client can't find your Web site—and search engines only "see" words (or copy). Remember that the clients only want to know what's in it for them, so tailor your Web pages to answer that question. Keep it simple, and not overly wordy. Avoid using industry jargon and lingo that most people won't understand. The goal is to give them enough information to encourage them to decide to call you for an in-depth conversation about their project. Hire a copywriter, and work with them to polish the final message. Then, have friends and family read that message, and get their opinion on readability, persuasiveness, etc. before you post it to your site.

Clients and Access

It is important to make sure that your Web site is easy to navigate, with links to other pages from anywhere on the site. It is also a good idea to allow clients to contact you from every page. Have a "contact page," but also include links to e-mail and phone numbers on every page. Make it easy for people to get in touch without searching. Your site should be updated regularly with new projects and information. There is nothing worse than outdated and irrelevant information still hanging around. This is why you want to be able to make changes without going back to your Web designer.

To increase its interactive value to my clients, my site uses a password-controlled client access page, which allows the building team and the client to track progress of their project from anywhere. The Web designer also added a link from my site to Basecamp HQ for their project management service. This is appealing to clients who are traveling or who live in other areas. It is also useful for the building and design team to stay in contact, assign tasks, archive documents, etc.

Take the time to understand your business goals and who your ideal clients are. Work with a good Web designer to build your Web site around them. Let your site have a "personality" that reflects your company values. People will consequently feel like they know you and, when they call you, they will be that much closer to hiring you. After all, isn't that the ultimate goal of having a Web site!

It's amazing to think that launching a Web site was newsworthy back in 1993, but when we launched ours in Baltimore, we sent a press release to the newspaper and thought that would be that. What we got was front-page coverage in the business section and a ten-paragraph story about how we were the only designers in the Baltimore region to have a Web site. Talk about free advertising!

BRANDING YOUR BUSINESS

Now that we've got you plotting innovative advertising campaigns, let's spend some time with advertising's smoother older brother, branding, as he's the spirit behind the marketing operation. No, we aren't talking about branding cattle; we're alluding to the process of developing an image for your business that can be conveyed through your marketing initiatives. Technically speaking, branding is the promotion of a particular product or company by means of advertising and distinctive design.

If you are anywhere close to being successful, you and your business will become a brand. After all, that's what we designers do: We sell ourselves as much as we sell our designs. It all goes hand in hand. Believe it or not, you already are a brand. Today, everyone is in some way. Perhaps we learned it from our culture, but your personal brand can be seen in everything you do. It's where you're seen and whom you're seen with, and shines through:

- In the way you act and dress
- In the car you drive
- In the words you use
- In the business cards you hand out
- In your letterhead
- In your Web site

We hope you realize that in order to make it, you and your evolving brand must be consistent even while you're dodging daggers on your first run through the designer gauntlet. Yes, you're going to be scrutinized and picked apart by some of your competition, so it's important that you don't give them any unnecessary ammunition.

Every time you're in the public eye, you have to be able to project a genuine energy, which means that most of the time you really have to feel it. So tighten your ship, because you're telling the world about your brand every day through your personal appearance and behavior.

Breathe In an Established Air

So, what does a successful interior design brand mean to you? Being stylish? Talented? Skilled? Competent? Established? Yes to all of those, but if you ask us, being established is the most important—particularly in starting your business. As a young design entrepreneur, you must present an established air from the get-go, because you want people to believe you've been around forever.

Believe us, if your office has been around for a year, people will think you've been there for three. If you've been around for two years, they will think you've been there for ten. And if you've been around for seven years, they'll think you've been there forever! (People personally think we've been here on the Monterey Peninsula "forever," because in the beginning, they saw so much of us in print and on TV. The reality is, we moved to Carmel only nine years ago.)

Image Is Everything

As you might imagine, we are firm believers in maintaining a fabulous image in order to attract "our type" of clientele. That's why we believe developing your brand image should be high on your priority list at this stage in your career. No successful designer goes through life without spending a lot of time honing his or her brand image. You won't be able to get away with not paying attention to your image in the public eye, either.

So, start working on your image today by reading books and attending seminars that will help you better understand the essence of branding. The goal is for you to learn to cultivate a brand image that supports your work and attracts your type of clientele.

Brands That Stand Out in a Crowd

Each designer has his or her own "story" for branding, and that's great. Do some research and find one that is perfect for you. Some designers feel strongly that your brand should distinguish you from the competition. With that in mind, how can you go about making your brand a head above the rest? Here are some suggestions:

- Try developing a mystique for your brand

- Have a compelling story that you sincerely want to tell

- Be consistent in the presentation of your brand

Once your image is in place, your marketing machine will enhance your story so that people will begin to notice you. As for differentiating yourself from the pack, that might be hard in the beginning, especially in today's arena in which everything goes, but standing out is still a function of great marketing and positioning. Sure, it would be nice to separate from the pack, but not at the cost of appearing flakey or extreme.

Keep in mind that if you are targeting middle-class clients, you don't have to have a high-class image. You should conjure a more populist brand in order to attract "your kind" of people. Your image must match your brand, so dress appropriately. It simply drives us crazy to see designers in big hats and outrageous jackets, because it totally distracts from the business.

You can't always live like your clients, but you at least need to look like you fit in. Smart young designers who target older clients must adjust their dress code. No matter where they come from, older clients are by definition more conservative. Translation: do not dress trendily.

Also, don't shop at a store known for low prices and low-quality clothes and still expect to "dress to impress." A designer must show a real sense of style that says, I understand my client is about to spend a lot of money. That means a designer's entire "look" (be it dress, actions, or designs) should be built to last.

Dress for Success

Since my (Tom's) mother was a costume designer, one thing I've always known how to do is dress. When we were starting our business in the 1970s, we didn't have a lot of money, but one thing we did have was a wardrobe.

At the time, we were extremely preppy and living in Philadelphia when it was very conservative, so it was important for us to convey an image that was pulled together, was coordinated, and matched. Our preppy look worked for us. Now, as we've gotten older, our dress has become our signature look and affects the way we are widely perceived.

The lesson here is that you don't have to be a trendy dresser to stand out in the crowd. Let your work distinguish you from your clients and peers. Challenge yourself by developing a look that is as timeless as your brand so that it has the legs to last at least another ten years.

We know what some of you hotshots are thinking. After all you've learned, you want to brand yourself as a "hot new designer." Good idea, but it's a bit more complex than that. Sure, hot designers come along from time to time, and without question, marketing plays a major part in their meteoric rise. But it doesn't happen overnight, and it never has. What most people don't realize is all the time, effort, and money that go into a campaign to burst onto the scene. There is absolutely no such thing as a hot designer popping on to the scene without a lot of planning, resources, and luck.

So, while you dream of attaining rock star status, work on your marketing plan, get out there, and meet your destiny with a smile on your face. Then maybe, just maybe, if you have a clever mix of good advertising, innovative marketing ploys, and a clear idea of how to position yourself in the marketplace, in time you may become that hot new designer who appears to the outside world to have magically burst onto the scene.

CASE STUDY: POSITIONING AN EAST COAST LUXURY BRAND

Every young designer has to decide how, when, and where to present him- or herself to the public. This is what's called "positioning." It is essential for designers to understand that when you position yourself somewhere (like at an event or within a certain social or professional circle), you are aligning your brand with that image. Be careful and consistent with your positioning, because you are not just presenting yourself as an individual. You are presenting yourself as a professional brand.

Cultivating a Brand

At twenty-five or thirty years old, the world looked a lot different to us than the world we see at (gasp!) nearly sixty years of age. The same can be said for our brand, but even in the early part of our careers, we knew for certain that we wanted to work in the upper end of the luxury residential market. So, what did we do to cultivate a professional brand that would get us there?

As you know, we decided our brand would be one of upwardly mobile young "preppies" with genteel backgrounds of wealth and privilege. We immediately transformed the way we dressed, the way we ran our personal affairs, where we lived, what we drove, and how we interacted with those around us.

These changes weren't lies—we never said anything but the truth as far as schooling and upbringing were concerned, but it was building "the image" that was important.

Branding, Positioning, and Networking

To show off our shiny new brand image, we began to think of ways to position ourselves in order to attract the type of clients we were targeting with our business. Since we were interested in doing high-end luxury residential, we decided to skip the gun shows and the monster truck rallies and began attending the theater, ballet, opera, and symphony, all of which we truly enjoyed.

We bought tickets in the area of the theater where the other young professionals mingled, and during the intervals, we were always in the lobby, looking fabulous. As we networked, we started being noticed by other professionals and began to be invited to the "right" parties and charity events. Why? Because we had the right image, brand, and positioning, and we looked and acted like we belonged.

Brand Impacts Everything

And so it was, from that point on; we were invited to participate in our first show house, and from that, our first larger, more important projects came to us. It certainly didn't happen overnight, and neither will your brand. Each of these steps happened over a period of time, so know you won't become a household name in six months. It takes time to build a brand, shape it, and then put it into action.

Of course, some designers will break out earlier than others, but take into account that it was most likely their commitment to their professional brand that was one of the biggest determining factors in their early success. We know this because our brand impacted every facet of our burgeoning business. It affected how people talked about us in conjunction with our business practices. Our brand was what the press came to talk to us about when our first interviews came along. Our brand is why it was an easy transition to build our business into the luxury Carmel brand we have today.

Finding and Committing to Your Brand

Your brand can be based on anything you want, but you have to have a clear idea of what ideas or images you would like to conjure in the public eye. Ask yourself what words exemplify your design business. Some of ours are tailored, sophisticated, and "architectural" in feeling, meaning that we generally prefer clean lines and don't do the "fussy" look. Try to find the right words that best describe your business; it is a great way to get your internal conversation started.

Once you find your brand, keep in mind that branding takes a commitment to "being the brand" every single day of your life. You have to be consistent. If you are indeed going into luxury residential design, then you can't show up at your client's home driving a Toyota. It has to be a late model automobile. Back in the day, our car of choice was a Volvo; now, in Carmel, it's a Jaguar. You had also better not be using $14-a-yard Robert Allen fabrics!

Build an image, then stick to it. That's what Martha Stewart did. It's also what some English kid named "Archibald Leach" did with his brand back in the 1930s, and look how it turned out for him: he created the "Cary Grant" movie star image that the world still recognizes today.

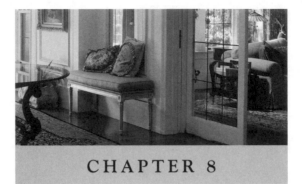

CHAPTER 8

HOW TO ATTRACT CLIENTS

Selling Yourself in the Design World

"Whether you think that you can or you can't,
you are usually right."

—HENRY FORD

Now that you budding entrepreneurs have donned your designer hard hats and are in the midst of constructing a fundamentally sound blueprint for your future, don't think for a minute that once you've mastered business modeling and the sublime art of the sizzle (i.e., marketing, advertising, and PR), you're automatically on the road to design prosperity. Not so fast, young whippersnappers! First, it's time to discover the qualities inside you that are going to insure your success.

AWAKEN YOUR INNER SALESPERSON

Let's not forget about another essential piece in the entrepreneurial puzzle that must be solved before launching any successful design firm: the development and mastery of one's own sales techniques. Did any of you romantics really think you were getting into this business to be an artist? Please. You're here to ply your trade (i.e., make money), so prick up your ears; this will be on the final exam.

Some of you naïve souls reading this book may still argue that interior design as an art form has nothing whatsoever to do with sales, and that may be true on some distant planet. But if you step back and look at interior design as a business, you will see that offering your services for pay goes hand in hand with being a designer. That said, it's amazing to see how many young, talented designers these days have problems selling themselves. We've come to the conclusion that some people just don't "get" the concept of sales. As for us, we're firm believers that it's really not that difficult if you put your mind to it.

Here's a jumpstart for you nonbelievers, so grab a pen and write this down, and then Velcro it to the inside of your brain: Your sales skills are just as important as your design abilities. This notion may be shocking to some, but when you get out there in the real world, you'll soon be humming our tune. Some of you are saying, "But guys, I'm an exceptionally talented designer; I work really hard; I have a fancy design degree, a wonderful pedigree, decent resources, and extraordinary resolve. My work is going to sell itself, right?" Wrong. Very, very wrong.

In America, the art of sales is king. No matter how striking your design talent, no matter how many connections you have in the industry or how hard you work creating mind-blowing designs, the truth is that your sales technique, otherwise known as your salesmanship, is going to be the "mojo" that convinces every one of your clients to "sign on the dotted line." So get used to it: sales is here to stay.

Sales Is Not a Four-Letter Word

"Sales" as a concept may have a bad image in some arty circles, because it doesn't sound "cool" and implies a "sucker" is being sold a bill of goods he or she doesn't want. But if you ask us, we love the sales aspect of the design game. After all, we're consumers, too! We love to shop (for ourselves and our clients) and know that every purchase we make isn't forced on us by some slimy salesperson.

Sometimes we, like everyone else, want to be sold something.

Along those lines, how can you discount the efforts of a designer who is aggressively selling his product to clients who love what they're buying?

We certainly can't, and neither should you. If we can slap a little more practical sense into you, know this: In the twenty-first century, you must be able to sell yourself to succeed in any line of business. So get with the program, liberal arts undergrads, or retreat into the corduroyed confines of academia.

Newsflash: You're in it for the Money

If you're still not sold on the "icky sales part" of the design business, think long and hard about whether it's beneath you to:

- Promote your own designs through innovative marketing
- Develop an innovative design product for a needy public
- Talk shop with existing and prospective clients in social settings

- Genuinely show how your business can meet any client's unique needs
- Present designs that deftly blend style, form, and function to create beautiful living spaces

All of these actions are "selling" just as much as asking for money, which, by the way, is why we are in business. We need to earn a living, remember? You may not think you're in it for the money, but believe us, you are. In this world, cash provides freedom and you, being the fabulous designer you are, must be free to do what it is you do so well.

If you are looking for objective guidance on this matter by running with some of the glamorous decorette designers on the scene today, take heed. You're going to find that many of them don't "get" the sales aspect of the design game at all. Due to their lives of wealth and privilege, selling is not a concept with which they have been presented. That's not what "ladies who lunch" do.

For the rest of us, if the sales process bothers you in some way (morally, ethically, whatever), you really must find a way to embrace what you may forever consider "the dark art of the sale" as soon as possible. If you do not, be warned: You will never make it in the modern design world.

DESIGNING YOUR SALES PHILOSOPHY

Has your design universe expanded considerably? That's what universes do—they expand. In the flash of an eye, you're not only an interior designer and an aspiring entrepreneur; you're also a project manager, a marketer, and a sales maestro. Nothing's ever simple, is it? If you step back, you will see that every piece of the entrepreneurial puzzle is interconnected, like a great big ball of rubber bands.

We hope you're up to the challenge, because now, it's time to start thinking about a sales philosophy that you truly believe in for your business. That's right; you've got to believe it yourself, so no trite "sales patter," please.

Developing, and truly believing in, your own personal sales philosophy is what's going to separate you from all the disreputable salespeople in the design world. Take careful consideration in developing your own philosophy, as it should represent your company's values and define what your design business means to you and your clients.

We know some of you would love to have your hand held right now, but we frankly can't tell you what your sales philosophy should be. Instead, you'll have to look inward and do some soul-searching. And if you really want to learn more about sales, you should consider taking a few business courses at a university or junior college.

We believe a great deal in the value of a business education, particularly for interior designers. One of us (Tom) even teaches a business practices course at Monterey Peninsula College. The art of business and the practice of design are intricately interconnected.

The Consummate Salesperson

If you took our course, you'd get a taste of our business philosophy while discovering our belief that a consummate salesperson is elegant in approach, gentle in persuasion, and tender in success. Great salespeople don't gloat about how much they charge per project. Great sales is about how you feel knowing you pleased your valuable client and, at the same time, helped pay your child's college tuition. That's what we call "warm fuzzies" for everyone. That is success.

If you're struggling to come up with your philosophy, here are a few pointers to get started. In brainstorming, it may help to include a few of our "golden rules" for a successful design salesperson:

- Present the best possible solution to any design dilemma
- Have integrity in pricing and in making promises to the client
- Be professional in demeanor, disposition, and outlook
- Be adaptable and diplomatic in all your business dealings
- Be enthusiastic, creative, and driven to sell yourself 24/7

If you pattern your game plan after ours, adhering to these five suggestions, you'll find that our golden rules usually result in positive real-world sales practices, such as:

- Having a great elevator speech
- Having excellent greeting techniques
- Having a positive approach
- Fostering new client relationships
- Becoming a great listener
- Presenting compelling design concepts to clients
- Conveying your vision to your team of business allies
- Managing a project from start to finish
- Giving everyone credit, clients included

Hale-Williams: Born to Sell

Could sales possibly be that simple? Maybe...or maybe not. Moses had ten commandments, and although we only have five, you are the variable in our equation for success.

Now that you're on the road to discovering your own sales philosophy, we hope you aren't disappointed to learn that salesmanship is a skill we learned at a much earlier age. One of us (Tom) had a father who was a traveling salesman from just after World War II until he retired at the age of seventy. He was able to impart a lot of wisdom about meeting people and working with a true sales philosophy. The other one of us (Robert) "cut his teeth" growing up in the hotel (hospitality) business, where he learned the importance of working with people and service. Once he went to work for British Airways, he learned the art of corporate sales.

After "cutting our teeth" in sales as young boys, once we got into the design business, it seemed like a natural thing to sell. Not to "toot our own horn," but now we're so good at it, we have trouble distinguishing selling from any other type of conversation. We sell ourselves all the time without the presentation looking forced. You would do well to follow suit.

But how does one go about doing it? Not to get too "New Agey" on you, but good salesmanship is really a state of mind. Once you get your feet wet, you'll find that one of the biggest keys to success is your belief in the product and service you are selling. If you truly feel comfortable with your offering, it will go a long way toward making it easy to sell your interiors.

FISHING FOR NEW CLIENTS

Now that you've done your research, identified your target market, and have your sales philosophy percolating on the front burner, where exactly—and on whom exactly—do you intend to hone your sales techniques?

A wise and fabulous person once said it doesn't matter how hot your "sales chops" are; the only thing you're going to catch is a cold if you aren't fishing in the right pond. We know you're hungry, so the first thing you should know is that in the design game, referrals are king. A referral is another way of saying that a person (a client, a friend, an associate, or a colleague) has recommended you to a potential client. Obtaining referrals and subsequently prospective clients is all about positioning, preparation, and timing; or, in other words, being the right designer, in the right place, at the right time.

Be a Design Detective

In drumming up business, every designer should put on his or her fedora and trench coat and have some fun getting into the role of the design detective. You've done your market research; you know what your clients look like, how they think, and where they spend their time, so get out there and pound the pavement. Start marketing yourself and your business. Talk to people. It may help to think of your target client as a missing person who you've been hired to track down.

Here is a hot tip from a couple of insiders: The best leads come from client referrals. Start your investigation by thumbing through your client Rolodex (if you have one) to gauge whether you have any untapped leads sitting right under your nose. Think about those you know (directly or indirectly) who may be able to refer you to a client who fits your "missing person" profile. Then, make contact.

More often than not, you can find more work from the clientele you already have. This is because any residential client who hires an interior designer will create buzz among his or her friends that can lead to you getting more business. It's like the designer domino effect. The notion may seem fuzzy while you're still "wet behind the ears," but give it time and follow up on every lead, and you may uncover a few juicy prospects.

We don't have to tell you that the best referrals come from satisfied customers. We also shouldn't have to tell you that most clients would never hire an interior designer unless that designer had been recommended by a person they trust. So, stay in contact with happy clients after you have completed a project. Let them know how proud you are of their space and that you are interested in working with any of their friends who like your work.

Never look at any client relationship as an individual project. Rather, view it as the initial tapping of a vast well that could provide gushers of new clients down the road. Remember, clients talk. Every project should be considered a stepping-stone to the next big project.

The Referral Landscape

Of course, if you have no clients, don't despair. We all have to start somewhere. Here are a few leads to some alternative client streams in your area that are stocked with lots of prospects. Just make sure to bring your sales "mojo," your fishing rod, and some live bait, because the fish are biting.

Non-client referral streams can be found through referrals from:

- Friends and relatives
- Business allies
- Professional networking functions
- Social networking functions
- Industry colleagues

Now that you have an idea of the referral landscape, take one lesson we learned from our fathers to heart: The best clients are the ones who last a lifetime. That means that as young designers who are still developing, it is essential that you search for the type of client who suits your style so you can build an enduring relationship.

The goal is to foster relationships in which both you and the client can envision a lifetime of design decisions being made collectively. Flakey, bottom-feeding, or fly-by-night clients should never be your target market. We aren't telling you how to run your business, but when it comes to clientele, you should aim for wealthy and older clients.

Keep Putting Yourself Out There

You should also never stop aiming high. It's a common mistake for young designers to get busy, let their guard down, and stop selling. Never get so shortsighted or full of yourself as to believe you no longer have to sell your business 24/7. As soon as you think new clients will come strolling in based on your reputation or your healthy client base, guess what? They won't.

A trance channeler we met back on the East Coast once taught us a valuable lesson that can be summed up in a simple phrase: Put yourself out there, and good things will happen. Whatever you put out in the universe will come back to you, in some way.

Consistently putting yourself in the marketplace is extremely important for success in the interior design field. Although "aggressive" may be too strong a word, certainly, "persistent" and "determined" describe what you need to be to sell yourself and your business. So be visible, do outstanding work, and foster relationships with your design industry "friends." You'll find that some of them will refer you to prospective clients. The connections are like a big, bouncing ball of rubber bands that can be a lot of fun once you get the hang of it.

Stay Flexible, Within Reason

In attracting new clients, you should also be aware that saying "no" limits your career. Never say you're "not sure," especially when you are starting out. For example, a client comes into your studio and says, "I have a day spa. Do you do day spas?" A savvy young designer with confidence may have the audacity to say, "Well, I've never done a day spa before, but I know I can do it. My foundation in doing residential bathrooms will enable me to transfer my experience from residential to a commercial day spa environment. I want to be considered for the project."

Don't be afraid to occasionally have the tenacity to say "yes." That said, daring to dream can be a slippery slope for some of us with blind ambition. There are times when neophytes must have the restraint to say, "No—I'm not ready." If you can develop an uncanny ability to know the difference between a calculated gamble and a desperate leap, you will be light-years ahead of your competition when it comes to landing the type of clients that are right for you.

THE FIRST CLIENT INTERVIEW

At this point, hopefully, your detective work has paid off handsomely. If you've set up a first interview with a prospective client, congratulations! Keep in mind that the initial interview is your client's first chance to see you in person. Conversely, this is also your first opportunity to evaluate the client.

Before you go into your meeting, we suggest you keep digging. Find out as much information as you can about the prospect. Any personal or professional information will help. If your prospect was a referral, talk to your contact. If you know someone who knows your client, ring him or her up and probe your source with a smile. You'll be surprised what you can find if you ask the right questions.

The goal is to accumulate all the information you've gathered in a client dossier so you have a better idea of whom you are meeting. The last thing you want to do is go into your first interview cold and clueless.

Don't Over-Prepare

Many established designers will admit to being "over-prepared" when it comes to executing a project, as if being a "stickler" is a trait that's a prerequisite to putting together a space on time, on budget, and to the client's liking. But when it comes to meeting with clients, you "type A" personalities have got to learn how to relax a bit and improvise.

Quite a few young designers have been known to make the mistake of over-preparing for a client meeting. How is that a bad thing? Over-preparation has a tendency to make a young designer rigid and unable to flow with a new client's multiple trains of thought. In addition, over-prepared greenhorns tend to freak out if they make a mistake. They miss a mark, and voila—they're noticeably flustered and have lost their edge.

It's Showtime, Folks!

Our advice for you is to know your material but never rely on notes. So much of what we do is extemporaneous. Know your material, then be prepared to improvise your sales pitch, shake up the telling of it a bit, and customize the pitch to your client so it's always different and fresh. Have fun playing your form of interior designer jazz with your clients. Onstage is when you shine.

Once you're ready to sit down with your prospective client, you would do well to memorize a few handy bullets for navigating your first client interview. Don't write them down; memorize them. Then, go be that dynamic, persuasive, intelligent, competent, professional, charming, and human designer you know you are. Now that it's showtime, here are some suggestions for making the most out of your first meeting:

- Ask about the client's wants and needs
- Listen carefully
- Ask about the client's influences, and what they like
- Stay neutral at all times
- Take cues from the client's body language
- Let clients lead you and tell you what they want
- Hold off on giving your design opinion
- Ask about how the client feels about the project
- Ask clients to think holistically
- Ask clients to elaborate
- Talk about a ballpark budget

Your goal in the first meeting should be to determine whether you connect with this person. First impressions can be very insightful, so what do you think?

- Can you establish a rapport?
- Does this client have a personality you can work with?
- Do you like this person?
- Do you like the project itself?
- Does the client fit your target profile?

Don't ask us! Only you know the answers.

The client interview really can be a fun, creative process, and it's actually why we got into this business. We truly enjoy what we do, and we hope you will, too.

HOW TO QUALIFY A CLIENT

At this point, assuming your client is still interested in procuring your design services, as a smart designer, you should take a breath, step back, and think about whether this client is for you.

Your client may be gaga for you (and that's great), but one of the biggest mistakes young designers make right out of the chute is choosing the wrong type of clientele. Poor choices are usually made out of desperation.

We can't fault a designer for wanting to eat, but for heaven's sake, be careful in choosing who you're essentially "getting into bed" with. We've heard far too many horror stories from suckers who agreed to work with clients who are:

- Tightwads who complain about every penny spent
- High-maintenance lunatics who take up all your time and cause endless headaches with their controlling personalities

Why not leave inappropriate clients for other designers and try to find clients who are right for you? Remember, the client isn't the only one who has a say in the arrangement. You are the one who defines your own boundaries. During the entire courting process, designers should be closely examine the actions of potential clients to determine whether they are people they would want to work with over an extended period of time.

In deliberating his or her case, every designer should be aware of several obvious client "tells" that, in nine out of ten cases, prove to be harbingers of dreadful things to come for everyone involved. What's a "tell," you ask? It's a term gamblers use that means an unconscious behavior that betrays an attempted deception. Although the word "deception" may be a bit harsh for the world of interior design, give your potential client our Hale-Williams Client "Tell" Rundown (outlined below), and see if any of these "tells" strike a chord.

Does Your Client Make Eye Contact?

Clients have to look you in the eye. Why? It's a sign of respect, and it builds trust among businesspeople. You'll find that good clients have a certain energy in their communications with you. By that, we mean a real interest in the process and what's going to happen. If you can't feel the love, then by all means, run for the hills.

Does Your Client Have a Sense of Humor?

A sense of humor is vital. If the client has no sense of humor about the project and how it will play out, we will not take the job. There will be times when humor will help you move the project forward and keep the client happy and on track.

Is Your Client into Horror?

Another red flag is when clients immediately get into telling horror stories about other designers. If you run into one of these clients, think long and hard about whether or not you want to work with this person. You could be the next celebrity guest on their "hit" parade.

Have You Seen the House?

Always look at the state of the home when you interview. If it is well-kept and clean, that's a good start. If we are invited to look at the bedrooms and find clothes on the floor, believe it or not, we will not take the job. This is because a messy home is a sign of an unorganized client who is unable to make decisions. He or she may be the kind of person who allows a project to languish in the doldrums of dead-end design jobs. We may sound rigid here, but trust us: If the house isn't well-kept, take a walk.

Is Your Client Talking Turkey Too Soon?

This one needs no explanation. If pricing and cost are worked into the conversation more than three times within our first visit to the site, we will not take the job. The drawn-out version of the same syndrome is a client who is unable to come to an agreement regarding the budget. These are definitely red flags!

Does Your Client Know How to Listen?

More than anything in this world, as a young interior designer, you want a client who is willing to listen to your ideas. A client who listens is more inclined to give you the personal information you need to build a customized vision for his or her home. This creates an ideal situation for you as a designer.

THE CLIENT PRESENTATION

Let's assume your answers to all of the questions in the Hale-Williams Client "Tell" Rundown above are resoundingly positive. You like the project, and the prospective client is interested in learning more about what your firm can do for them. Now, pat yourself on the back for a minute, collect a retainer, and then schedule another meeting, *pronto*. It's time you started preparing for an official presentation.

The presentation is designed to take your client along the road to fulfillment. At this point, you have already created the space planning, made color and fabric selections, and found just the right furniture and lighting. What's next?

Although every designer has a different presentation style, here are eleven universal suggestions that have worked for us for a combined fifty-four years. We call them the "eleven commandments of client presentation." You really should digest these nuggets before you start running around with your hair on fire.

1. Make Your Pitch Tight

Unlike the first client meeting, some serious preparation is in order before making a presentation. That's not to say there isn't any room for improvisation, but avoid unloading any killer surprises (other than the "hairy armpit"—more on him later) in presenting to clients.

As far as developing concepts, we simply don't have the space to explain our process or the sublime method to our madness. Suffice it to say we reflect long and hard on the client's needs as well as how we can best address those needs with our designs. In putting a presentation together, know that the best presentations aren't flashy. They are airtight and carefully prepared so that they can be delivered in a calm, direct manner.

2. Be Prepared For Everything

During your presentation, be prepared:

- To have an open dialogue
- To ascertain the scope of the project
- For the client to ask a lot of questions
- For you to ask a lot of questions
- To take clues from the client's appearance and body language
- To be a keen observer
- To read client reactions to ideas
- To ensure all your selections are current and in stock

3. Don't Overstay Your Welcome

We highly suggest you put a limit on your meeting time. Allow between one and two hours for a presentation. And, since most sales include a presentation, we try not to let it last for more than ninety minutes. We've noticed that clients tend to lose focus after ninety minutes, anyway, and by then, everyone is a little overwhelmed and needs to get away from the meeting for awhile. Try sticking to two hours or under on most presentation meetings.

4. Segment Presentations

Make sure to organize your presentations based on exactly what you plan to present. If the presentation is for an entire residence, divide the presentation into rooms; that way, there is a natural flow to how the project unfolds.

For larger projects that require several meetings to discuss, divide them into segments and present them one at a time. For example, one day you may present your concepts for the public spaces; during the next meeting you'll present concepts for kitchens and baths; and in a third meeting you will present your bedroom concepts. Breaking a project up into segments allows the designer to keep the ninety-minute rule in place while not wearing out the client.

5. Leave the Romance for the Bedroom

We know you're going to be bored with us, but while some designers like to seduce clients with lavish visuals and romantic images for their living space, we say, Leave the romance for the bedroom. This is business, and we are thus personally very straightforward about what will be done. When it comes to style, to each his own; but if you ask us, you should be careful not to get too romantic.

We've found plain, old education—not romantic imagery—to be the biggest part of an effective presentation. This is in part because most clients don't have a clue as to what designers do for a living! Don't be surprised to find that you, in fact, are the first designer with whom your client has ever dealt. Be prepared to explain the process. It is important that you are able to speak the client's language as best you can, so that he or she understands what your pitch truly means. Remember, when clients nod their heads endlessly, it doesn't necessarily mean they get it.

6. Limit Your Concepts

We generally present between two and four concepts for any space. The presentation includes furniture choices, fabrics, and finishes. Concepts aren't fleshed out with prices, but we always try to have a general idea of where the pricing is going.

One conceptual trick is to present the client with an idea that we call "the hairy armpit." This idea that we present is something we know isn't right for the client. We're actually looking for them to refuse the concept by telling us "no." It's the "no" word that is most important. Once they say "no" to us and find that the sky doesn't fall, they are far more willing to be truthful about other decisions. This "hairy armpit" trick usually loosens clients up so that we can move more freely into the production phase.

7. Encourage Participation

Having the right tools in your studio is very important when you make a sale. We have a large worktable on which we present our projects to clients (fifty-four inches wide by seventy-two inches long by thirty-six inches high). It's a fabulous setting for working up projects, and encourages client participation because it has lots of space to push fabrics and things around in order to get a holistic picture of the entire project.

We generally show large fabric, carpet, and wall covering samples (rather than small samples) and overlay all the colors, fabrics, and finishes to create a more comprehensive look on the worktable. To the surprise of some, we have never done full boards for our clients. We believe our business is just too tactile for that. Full boards may work in commercial design but, in our opinion, not in residential design.

8. Be Fluid and Adaptable

One of the reasons we insist upon presentations in our office is that it gives us the ability to make changes on the spot. Here at Hale-Williams Interiors, we have our full library at our fingertips. Should the client not like a selection, for whatever reason, we put it aside and start reselections on the spot. We can change almost any selection and, in this day and age, there are far too many choices to try and force one down a client's throat.

As an aside, our clients love to watch the process and see us at work. Yours will, too. The presentation gives you and your client a chance to interact about what they are seeing. It is, after all, the client's home; what the client likes and how he or she reacts are very important.

9. Have a Feel for Price

Try to have a feel for where the price is going during most presentations. That way, there are no nasty surprises when you actually price out the designs. Do not disclose the price of the items as you go along. Wait until the end of the presentation or, even better, until the next meeting. That way, the changes that will almost always come up can be included in the finished pricing package.

10. Keep Going!

When you make a mistake during a presentation (and believe us, you will), move on and keep going. Many times, you're the only one who realizes you made the mistake. Real life has lots of mistakes. Try attending a Broadway play with talented, professional actors, and you'll see that even the best make mistakes at times. So, if you flub a line, keep moving forward. If the context is right, no one may even notice.

11. Know When to Fold 'Em

If, during your presentation, it is clear that you are not meeting the client's needs, try to end the discussion as gracefully as possible. Explain to the client your thoughts on another direction you might take, and ask a lot of questions to make sure you understand exactly what the client wants. Be sure to set the next presentation appointment at that time, and once the client has departed, get to work. If, at the next meeting, you find the client simply can't move forward, you might consider whether or not you wish to continue working with that client. This will be a very hard decision on your part, but in the end, releasing the client might be the best choice.

SELLING IS PART OF THE EQUATION

A designer who can't sell has no chance. Being able to sell yourself is a must if you expect to succeed. You won't get a decent job unless you can sell your talents and make people believe you know what you're doing. Sales is a vital part of this industry. The best names in design have always been great salespeople.

You have to remember, anyone can learn to do a presentation and make a sale, as we've discovered, but if you can't pull it together, that's fine. Find someone who can, and collaborate. It's essential that someone in your organization can meet and communicate with clients so that there is always a face and voice of the organization that clients can see and hear. The face of the organization helps tell clients what your firm is really all about.

Personality isn't everything. Some designers may not be outgoing in public, but they may be good one-on-one with a client. That's all it really takes in terms of securing clients, but never forget that designers communicate not only with clients, but with everyone involved in a project.

There are different levels in the industry, so be true to yourself, know what you do best, and then go and do it. If you're a rock star designer, you have nothing much to lose. But not everyone is a rock star designer, and thank goodness for that. If your personality is about technical components, maybe you don't want to be one of those flashy designers networking at the opera. Remember, in the majority of design circles today, it's all about form, comfort, and space.

The truth is, most of today's designers spend little time jetting around the world and more time in the office laying out design components for kitchen, bathroom, or closet systems to make sure all the pieces fit. To real-world designers, that's a design puzzle, and it's glamorous because it's what gets them excited.

If you go this route with your career, clients probably will not want a big sales pitch from you. Instead, they'll want a designer who can realize a functional vision and plug in components; nothing more, and nothing less.

There shouldn't be a million mini-sales in a project, but attention to the ongoing process is important. We suggest that you make contact with clients from time to time to update them on the process. These contact points are excellent times for add-on sales or expanding the project.

When the installations occur, make sure to compliment the client on his or her wonderful choices. We know, we know—*you* made the choices, but the client made the purchase. So, compliment the choice. Make them feel secure in their selections. We personally find this easy, because when we see the finished project for the first time, we're usually thrilled at the outcome and truly feel as if we all made the right choices.

ALWAYS BE CLOSING

If you didn't know before reading this chapter that everyone must sell in the real world, now you do. It doesn't matter if you're a natural salesperson or someone who learned the art of sales. When it comes to making money, having ability is not enough. You have to be consistent in your approach if you want to stand out in this dog-eat-designer-dog environment.

Have you noticed that successful people never seem to take their foot off the gas? To paraphrase the playwright David Mamet, good salespeople should ABC—always be closing. The best are always selling, because that's what they do. They don't know how to do anything else. They are always churning their roster and always looking for the next big client.

The best succeed not because they're the most talented, but because they want it more than their competition. Keep that in mind while you're busy churning your client list. Always be closing and ABF—always be focused—on the next project, the next referral. The goal, particularly for young designers like yourself, is to consistently land new clients who are better than your last.

CASE STUDY: GRADING ON A BELL CURVE

Every designer should understand that eye-popping talent, great sales technique, and a dogged approach to business development will not get you in the Winner's Circle every time. Even when you know you made an excellent presentation that meets all of your client's needs, temper your enthusiasm until the prospect signs a contract or letter of agreement.

The truth is, no designer lands every potential client. It just doesn't happen, so don't take it personally when it doesn't happen for you. Why can't a designer bat 1.000? Ultimately, it's always up to the client to decide, which makes interior design a vocation in which success ratios aren't guaranteed to any level of reasonable accuracy. Rejection is a part of our mysterious business. It happens to every designer, including us. Do you want proof?

A few weeks ago, we interviewed for a client we thought would be a perfect fit. It wasn't a large project; the client had moved into a new home in Pebble Beach and simply wanted to update drapery and add a few furniture pieces.

When we made contact, she complimented us on our showroom and on the fine reputation we had on the Monterey Peninsula. She mentioned two different friends who had spoken highly of our work and opined that we just might be the perfect fit for her smaller job. She had us purring like kittens. Of course, that was when the trouble started.

After our initial meeting, we visited her residence to take a look at what needed to be done. While she walked us through, she kept referring to what items had cost in Los Angeles and began asking what the pricing might be here in Carmel. She even had the nerve to question our fees, and you already know how we feel about that—three strikes, and you're out!

Her line of questioning implied that she felt we weren't as qualified as the L.A. designers with whom she had been working. To add insult to injury, she then questioned our pricing structure and said she "would let us know how she would work with us." Hey, now. Suffice to say, we weren't hired for the job. We suspect she thought we had the design chops but not the "pricing looks," but we don't really know. She never called back.

The lesson is: After all our years in the business, we still have a hard time accepting that we don't get every job. We wish we didn't let it bother us, but we're human, too. What gets us through the disappointment is stepping back and realizing how awful the project would have been had she hired us before we saw her true self. So, we choose to see the situation as moving us on to another audition. You should, too. There will always be another job out there. And it will probably be a better fit.

CHAPTER 9

SETTING UP YOUR DESIGN STUDIO

Getting It Right the First Time

> "Nothing so conclusively proves a man's ability
> to lead others as what he does from
> day to day to lead himself."
>
> —THOMAS J. WATSON

Some of you have traveled a long way on this journey: from wide-eyed neophytes scared to leap off the entrepreneurial high dive, to enthusiastic professionals courageously journeying down the business modeling rabbit hole. You've come a long way.

You've laid an early foundation for success by coming to terms with your segment, product, market, mission, and business objectives; you even found time to decide on a few pricing and sales philosophies that fit your style. Simply put: you're on fire. But don't start signing autographs just yet.

BORN TO RUN

While the cement dries on your foundation's first coat, let's gear up to talk about the nitty-gritty details that go into business modeling, like equipping your business and design studio for optimal efficiency. We aren't talking about redesigning your spare bedroom into a home office; we mean establishing the operational infrastructure of your business.

Sitting down to draw up a comprehensive business plan may seem like a bore to those of you who prefer instant gratification, but believe us, this real-world application matters. For all you skeptics out there, here's a well-publicized secret: Every acclaimed designer working today has a little "business junkie" inside.

We're not all scatter brained stereotypes, after all, so don't prepare like one! Understand the importance of adopting sound business practices,

141

build them into your infrastructure, and find a way to have some fun with your business model. After all, this is your baby you're creating, so it behooves you to add some zest to her upbringing.

Get excited about your dreams, do the research, talk to everyone you can, play music, pray, chant—whatever it takes to get your brain firing and your creative juices flowing. Remember, this is not brain surgery. Unless you're designing hospitals or firehouses, lives are not at stake, so ease up on the intense brow furrowing. There's no need to be nervous.

Although some designers—mostly loyalists to the industry's staid professional organizations—believe a couple of paperback design mentors like ourselves should only be teaching you ASID-approved curriculum by rote, we're not here to play by their rules. Imposing any strict guidelines on you is the last thing we want to do, particularly at this stage in your career.

In case you need a refresher, our mission is simple: to empower you with the straight "skinny" on the business side of the design industry so that you can march to the beat of your own innovative drum. We hear what some of you are saying: "Robert and Tom, you're teaching us the chords but not the music! Why?" Simply put, there is no sheet music in the design industry. You have to write your own tune.

While you let that one sink in, how about we begin our infrastructure conversation with a nuts-and-bolts talk about business operations, specifically:

- Where are you going to set up shop?
- What office tools and equipment do you need?
- What operations methods should you employ?
- What in-house human resources are out there?

OFFICE SPACE

Let's begin with where you'll be spending at least two thirds of your waking life: your design studio. Where should a young entrepreneur set up shop? There are three options: a business office, a home office, and a retail shop or showroom.

Ideally, your sublime studio space should be located in a well-lit professional area with plenty of foot traffic and lots of glass, preferably near green trees and well-kept landscaping. Clients should feel comfortable coming to your location and at ease in your space.

It doesn't hurt to plant yourself in a part of town where your clients naturally congregate, but your location doesn't have to be trendy. It simply must be in a place where clients feel comfortable visiting and spending money. At a minimum, try looking in an area where your clients are comfortable traveling and parking a car. If you are a luxury residential designer, avoid setting up shop in a down-market office park next to a freeway under an airport flight path.

When it comes to size, for an office that accommodates one to four designers, generally look for something between five hundred and one thousand square feet. If you're going larger, consider adding another 150 square feet per employee up to about eight or ten employees. After that, you're in the big-time, so your considerations are going to be based on what specialty you provide and how many extra employees you have.

The Business Office
Finding a business office space in a freestanding building, a design center, or a strip mall is one of the best locations for a new designer, as it immediately creates an aura of professionalism and respectability for your firm. The nice part of this setup is that it usually requires far less in rent than if you were to rent a commercial retail space. The downside is that you may not get quite as much foot traffic passing by your office.

Once you've found a space with potential, it's a good idea to check out the other tenants in the building or complex to see if you will fit in. Ideally, you'd like to be part of a professional community, so consider aligning yourself, at least location-wise, with lawyers, accountants, or other creative professionals.

The Home Studio
If you're looking to get started in a home studio, you have an easier decision to make, because you probably already live in the space where you want to start your business. In this scenario (the most popular for young design entrepreneurs, by the way), it goes without saying: when it comes to rent, the price is right, but there are still some things to consider before settling on a homebound operation:

- Is there enough room to run the business?
- Is there a place for you to have clients visit?
- Are you located in an area that looks like where your clients live?

If you answered no to any of those questions, you may want to seriously consider a commercial or retail office space for your business. Frankly, we aren't going to spend a lot of time on the pros and cons of a home office. Basically, we don't like this option. Although your finances may limit your ambition in this area, we suggest you do whatever you can to get your office out of your home as soon as possible. If you want to be a professional, you have to look and act like one.

The Commercial Retail Space

A commercial retail space is used primarily by design merchants who have on-site design offices, which are usually located in the back of the shop. Retail merchants sell retail products off their showroom floor, so if you're a retail designer who is interested in building a hybrid business model (similar to that of Tom's mother), you may want to consider renting a retail space. You're going to find that the cost of rent is more expensive; however, the payoff is more daily traffic passing your studio than if you were sitting in an office building or in your in-laws' bedroom.

Put Your Location to the Test

Once you've determined the type of space that's right for you, spend some time visiting all the choice areas in your market to decide where to position your business. When we moved from Baltimore to Carmel, we spent a week visiting six distinctly different retail areas.

We visited each in the morning between 8:00 and 10:00 a.m. to observe the traffic patterns. Then, we made the rounds during lunch to see how and where business was flowing. Finally, we made a third round between 3:30 and 5:30 p.m. to see if the trends we'd spotted were in any way different.

As it turned out, the location we originally thought would work was the one that tested the best. The office was in an up-market shopping village and was approximately eleven hundred square feet. It gave us enough room for our office, presentation space, and an area to display a small selection of upholstered furniture pieces we were representing, so we went for it. We must have caught lightning in a bottle, because we are still in the same location to this day.

EQUIPPING YOUR STUDIO

Now that you've gotten your studio and location mapped out, what is it going to take to turn your little slice of heaven from an empty commercial space into a hit factory for your design work? You will need tools, knowledge, equipment, and a few tricks of the trade. Let's start with the "stuff" first. What tools do you need? The most important tool is, of course, your design acumen. After that, your equipment should consist of the following:

- A desk for every employee
- A chair for every desk

- Filing cabinets
- A computer for every employee
- An Internet connection
- Software
- Stationery (letterhead, envelopes, cards)
- Shelves
- A presentation area
- A large table (to spread out materials)
- A library of samples
- Client books
- Client folders
- A small refrigerator and a coffee/tea maker
- Telephones with multiple lines
- An anwering machine or answering service
- A copier/printer/scanner/fax machine
- A client contract or letter of authorization template
- Blueprints, floor plans, and layouts

Most of your tools need no explanation, but we will elaborate on a few that are specific to interior design.

Your Library

Every designer takes pride in having a fabulous library of fabric samples and catalogues. You want to build as large of a library as possible to save time traveling to and from showrooms to source materials. Remember, time is money, and an in-house library saves immense amounts of both.

In putting your studio together, plan to install additional storage for your library, either in a separate room or by installing built-in cabinets and shelves. We have our sample library along the walls of our office that surround our meeting and showroom space, and it works fine.

Once you've installed your library shelves, how are you going to fill them? One way is to begin collecting samples, or memos, by contacting sales reps of product lines you wish to carry. You could also go into the showroom of the fabric house or furniture line you want to use and ask for help in creating a library of their product samples.

Most fabric and paper companies do not allow samples to be kept once they have been used for a project. You may even be required to buy some of your library samples. Instead of just keeping memos, which some designers notoriously do, talk to the rep about building a library of his or her product with the memos you have already brought into your library. Trust us: All of the companies out there, be they furniture, carpet, paper, or fabric makers, want designers to like their product. To that end, they will offer all sorts of help to start your library.

Accounting Software

It is important that you employ some brand of computer software for project and financial management. As for what kind, it's up to you to research what best fits your needs and helps you stay abreast of what's new. Today, one of the most affordable and easiest to learn is QuickBooks Pro.

QuickBooks, accounting software that helps manage your books and financial statements, allows you to determine, through multiple reports, the state of your business at any given time. It also gives you the ability to track time, generate payroll, work on taxes, and perform a plethora of other tasks. In the "old" days—before the 1980s—these jobs were done by office managers or accountants.

Management Software

If you're looking for software to help organize your myriad of project management tasks, software packages like Studio IT and Design Manager should be on your shopping list. Built specifically for interior designers, both accomplish the same functions as QuickBooks, while helping designers manage projects in a more refined manner.

Additionally, these software packages give you the ability to network with other designers in your office, which is not a bad idea if you intend to expand your firm beyond two or three employees. In the end, these software programs may require a longer learning curve, but if you ask most professional designers, it's worth the investment.

Phone Etiquette

We are continually amazed and appalled at how phones are answered these days. After so many bad experiences, we've almost determined phone etiquette to be a long-lost art. What a shame! In a world full of bad customer service providers, young designers should never fly by the seat of their pants when it comes to client contact points.

Establish basic call behaviors for your business. Trust us—a cordial phone voice will make a lasting impression on older, wealthy clients who also miss the way things were done in the old days.

The Hale-Williams policy is to answer within two rings, and to lead with the name of our company, then our name, if we choose. You don't have to get too complicated with your greeting. Go with whatever method suits you, but be consistent in your approach. And for heaven's sake, be polite, be concise, be clear, and be consistent.

Leverage Your Voicemail

Don't forget about your company voicemail. One of those horribly robotic "The party you have dialed is not home…" messages is an easy way to kill a business and a career. At a minimum, make your outgoing message a human voice. And if you're an enterprising soul who's into leveraging untapped resources (and who isn't?), start thinking of your voicemail as free advertising space.

We are always looking for new ways to market our services, and we have found that spicing up our outgoing voicemail (by noting that we're award-winning residential interior designers and project managers) gives potential clients one more opportunity to learn about what we do. So, feel free to toot your own horn by adding some marketing sizzle to your script. Remember, this is still show business.

Some crafty designers have even been known to go as far as to enlist a friend with a sophisticated European accent to leave their outgoing message for them. Be prepared for your competition to try anything to enhance their brand! These are creative examples of how to take advantage of what tools you already have at your disposal. And let's face it: Mixing it up is more fun than simply stating the name of your company and asking the caller to leave a message.

The Letter of Agreement

Virtually every designer–client relationship is made official with a contract or letter of agreement (LOA) that's signed by both parties. In this CYA world, verbal agreements in any language don't cut it anymore. Most attorneys agree that there is no contract or letter of agreement written that guarantees against misunderstandings or disputes. What the letter or contract does is spell out what is expected from both designer and client.

Put this in your hard drive: Never—and we mean *never*—take a job without a signed contract or letter of agreement (LOA). You're just looking for trouble if you willingly wade into those murky waters at any point in your career. You can't afford to take this risk with *anyone*, and we're talking about friends, family, and lovers as well as more "typical" clients.

So, what does this document look like? A letter of agreement is a short, written explanation, usually consisting of one or two pages, that outlines the details of a project. These details may include:

- How the project will proceed (timing)
- How and when the client will be billed
- How the retainer or design fee will be billed out, and at what rate
- How proposals are prepared
- What type of deposit is needed to proceed with individual purchases
- An outline of the scope of the project, with specific details
- A determination of which rooms or areas are to be designed and included
- The details of how the design team will work with contractors and other service providers

Hale-Williams advocates LOAs over contracts, particularly for sole proprietors, because they do the job perfectly well and are easier to navigate and agree upon. When you're ready to begin crafting your own LOA, try referencing the following example, then see if you can write one that suits the way you run your business.

Sample LOA Form

September 3, 2008
Mrs. Susie Client
1000 Designer Way
Anytown, USA 10000

We are pleased to submit this agreement for design consultation of your new home at 1000 Designer Way. Any third-party services by (among others) architects and engineers should be engaged directly by the client. Wonderful Interior Design will work in coordination with any third-party interest hired by the client.

Wonderful Interior Design will be allowed to photograph the project with both before and after images to be used for promotion. The client's privacy will be ensured, and the images will remain the property of Wonderful Interior Design.

We would appreciate a nonrefundable design fee of $5,000 on your account. You will be charged $250 per hour for design work, including consultations, space planning, shopping, planning the project, production, and delivery. Travel time out of the area will be charged at a rate of 50 percent.

The fees will be billed up to the amount of the retainer. Should additional time be required, additional fees will be charged as agreed by the designer and client. You will be entitled to twenty hours of design time with the initial retainer. FedEx/UPS charges, if any, will be billed separately.

A written proposal will be prepared and presented to you for any purchases made through this office. Upon receipt of your written approval and a 60 percent deposit, your order will be placed. The balance of 40 percent is due before receipt or installation of goods.

As acceptance of this agreement, please sign and return a copy of this letter, along with a check for the retainer, to our office. We appreciate the opportunity to work with you on this exciting project.

Gloria Wonderful

Accepted _____ Date _____

Contracts

Many design firms use contracts, as opposed to LOAs, to cover all of the bases of a project. More complex than a letter of agreement, a contract is a comprehensive written agreement that drills into more facets of the project to detail exactly how it will be implemented.

The kinds of stipulations that can be included in a client–designer contract are endless. Let's just say that although a contract usually includes the contents of a letter of agreement, it also addresses "what if" scenarios. If you decide to use contracts, yours should include all the items you, the designer, feel are necessary to complete the project in a timely manner and address the needs of the client as far as completion is concerned.

If you are interested in contracts and want an example, take a look at the ASID contracts, which can be found in numerous publications and online. You might also want to review our sample LOA, then pick and choose the stipulations from those documents that you feel are most important to your business and your clientele. In addition, it may be a good idea to ask your lawyer whether a contract or an LOA would be most suitable for your particular business.

Business and Legal Forms

You should be familiar with the numerous forms needed to work with members of your profession and those contractors with whom you will work from time to time. Forms for budgeting, time scheduling, purchase logs, and estimate sheets are also needed in the office. A great resource is

Business and Legal Forms for Interior Designers (Allworth Press, 2001). You will also get used to signing contracts for everything from rent to an auto lease. Each time you special order furniture or other items, you are entering into a legal agreement, and many of these require signing some sort of contract form. There will be times when the services of your legal team will be invaluable, so don't hesitate to use them.

Drawings

At some point, a decision will have to be made regarding whether to create drawings in your office or to outsource the work to an outside architecture or design firm. Do your career a favor and, while you're young, learn to draw at least floor plans and layouts yourself. This skill is important because a designer who cannot draw floor plans already has a disadvantage in the marketplace. Why would you want to handicap yourself before the race has even begun?

Granted, unless you are an architectural designer, drawing up a full set of blueprints may be slightly out of your league. That's why we contract out to architects and builders, right? (This will be discussed in more detail in chapter 10, "Building Your Village.")

Blueprints

You may not have to draw blueprints, but if you want to be considered a true professional in this business, you have to understand how to read a full set of blueprints—that includes plans, elevations, cross-sections, electrical plans, reflected ceilings, finish schedules, and plot plans for the property lot. If you didn't learn how to read them in design school, learn to read them now. It's that important. If you aren't able to skillfully navigate your profession's road maps, you risk losing credibility with your team and your clients.

Floor Plans and Layouts

A floor plan or layout is a scale diagram of the arrangement of rooms in one story of a building. Not as detailed as blueprints, they are one of a designer's best friends. Often paired with wood or textile samples during client presentations, floor plans are used to illustrate the design and spatial look and feel of the finished project. Learn how to master the art of floor planning.

Drawing Tools

There is wonderful software available for every level of floor plan work. Whether or not you use some form of computer-aided design (CAD), the most popular software package, or work with a T-square and ruler (just kidding: no one uses a T-square anymore), you must have a place for storing large copies of blueprints, floor plans, and layouts.

We realize it is not always possible financially to buy a plotter large enough to produce blueprint-sized plans, but usually, your local print shop, Kinko's, or UPS Store will have the ability to print for you directly from an e-mail, storage disk, or zip-file. One final note: If you decide to do your floor plans in-house, be sure your CAD software is compatible with the ones used by your builders, contractors, and architects.

Final Tips on Setting Up Your Studio

Here are some additional suggestions to keep in mind in setting up your design studio:

- The success of your business will hinge on the location of your studio, so choose wisely.
- Choose a smaller office in the right area rather than a larger space in the wrong area.
- Don't "cheap out." Buy quality equipment (computers, software, etc.) from the start.
- If you cannot afford a lot of furniture for your space, buy a few quality pieces that will last rather than junk that has to be replaced every few years.
- Make sure your systems are in place before you open your doors.

SETTING UP YOUR BOOKS

Speaking of systems (since we're already inside your filing cabinet), let's talk about how you're going to "bless this mess" by setting up your paper trail, job books, resource file, and chart of accounts. We hope none of you is under the impression that just because a bunch of snazzy software packages exist, we're living in a paperless world. The truth is not even close.

If you are going to have a successful run as a design entrepreneur, the sad fact is that many trees will have to give their lives for the cause. Even with the help of advanced project management software, there are mountains of paper to be pushed daily, for any number of reasons.

Your Paper Trail

What is a paper trail, exactly? A paper trail is literally the written evidence of your business activities. Considering the hundreds of transactions that go into the procurement of goods and services, especially in the design industry, it should come as no shock that your firm's paper trail will play a giant role in the way you manage your projects.

The paper trail's most practical use is obviously for bookkeeping and tax purposes, but it also comes in handy when you need to review a transaction, develop a budget, or resolve a dispute. If there is a question from clients or vendors about what was ordered, received, or delivered, you have your paper trail to show exactly what happened. Remember, in business, nothing trumps the truth.

Would you believe we still employ a straightforward paper trail that doesn't involve a lot of high-tech computer technology? Oh, we love our software, but we still tend to do things the old-fashioned way. Why? As we said, there are so few transactions—even today—that are truly paperless. Everything we do in this industry is still done on paper (from ordering, invoicing, billing, etc.), and it would be nearly impossible for a single designer to go paperless while the design community has not.

We've always kept substantial hard-copy files. As for whether you should do the same thing, it all depends on the industry. If the design industry goes paperless, so will you. While we hold our collective breath and wait for that change, our advice is to brace your studio ahead of time for the (currently) inevitable paper avalanche by organizing a system that works for you.

Our paper trail captures more than numbers. We record everything pertaining to the project. Some designers may find this tedious, but it's essential. While some decorators place client orders while standing in line at Starbucks, we do it from our office and take notes, writing down the name of the person to whom we speak, the date and time of ordering, and so forth. When orders are done online, we make a copy of the final order.

Again, nothing beats the truth, so why not cover your tail every step of the way? It may seem like a pain at first, but once you get the hang of recording everything, you'll find that your due diligence will save hours of frustration in the long run. So, what are you waiting for? Get your paper trail going.

Your Job Books
You will need to organize your files. The filing system used by virtually every designer on earth to manage clients is called "job books" or "client files." Though your firm's books will be based on which system you use for accounting and project management (like QuickBooks Pro or Studio IT), keep in mind that even though all these systems do the job, you'll still want some sort of hard-copy client file in which to store samples, written notes, copies of proposals, and the like.

Most firms still employ old-fashioned ring binders with dividers to sep-arate different aspects of the project. You should, too. Assign one job book per client, and start filling yours with pertinent aspects of the job like:

- Samples
- Written notes
- Copies of proposals
- Blueprints
- The LOA
- Purchasing orders
- Tear sheets
- Billing invoices

Once you have all your project materials and information in one place, you're going to find that (voila!) you're able to manage your clients and projects more effectively. This organization also helps when clients ask questions about particular aspects of the job. With a flip of the wrist, you will have the answer at your fingertips.

Your Resource File

In addition to job books, every designer needs to create a resource file in which vital information for every member of your "village" (vendors, crafts-men, contractors, etc.) is stored. We're going to talk more about your village in the next chapter, but for now, know you can store this data on a spreadsheet or create a binder in which to keep your business cards and contact informa-tion. The point is to make all your resource information easily accessible.

If you're like most designers, you will probably have to churn your resource list for some time to test the efficiency of your contractors before you settle on a dream team. You don't have to be completely anal about constantly updating your list, especially if your resources keep turning over or if you live in a large city and have access to a design center. But if you're one of those brave souls who reside in remote areas like Alaska, where design resources are scarce, start your file now and keep it current.

The Chart of Accounts

While you're building your paper infrastructure, you, like every designer, should establish a chart of accounts to record all of your business's income and distributions. This may seem like a fundamental step to any rational businessperson, but you'd be surprised at how many designers fail to apply the most elemental bookkeeping procedures.

A chart of accounts is significant because it shows you where you are making and spending money. It also highlights what percentage of your distributions goes, for example, to rent, the electric bill, office expenses, advertising, promotions, auto expenses, furniture, accessories, etc. Here is a generic example of a chart of accounts:

Account	Type	Income Tax Line
1010 – First National Bank	Bank	
4010 – Loan from shareholders	Income	
4011 – Delivered sales	Income	
4012 – Wholesale delivered sales	Income	
4014 – Design fees	Income	
4015 – Commissions	Income	
4016 – Refunds	Income	
4020 – Showroom sales	Income	
4021 – Showroom rental income	Income	
5000 – Distributions	Expenses	
5010 – Showroom expenses	Expenses	
5011 – Commissions paid	Expenses	
5020 – Window treatments	Expenses	
5021 – Delivery, freight, etc.	Expenses	
5023 – Fabrics	Expenses	
5024 – Furniture	Expenses	
5025 – Reupholstering	Expenses	
5026 – Miscellaneous accessories	Expenses	
5027 – Wall covering	Expenses	
5028 – Installing window treatment	Expenses	
5029 – Carpeting	Expenses	
5050 – Contractor	Expenses	
5060 – Accounting	Expenses	
5070 – Advertising	Expenses	
5160 – Office expenses	Expenses	
5180 – Promotions	Expenses	
5190 – Research and development	Expenses	
5200 – Rent	Expenses	
5220 – Miscellaneous taxes	Expenses	
Accounts receivable	Acct. receivable	
Opening balance equity	Equity	
Sales tax payable	Other current liability	
Undeposited funds	Other current asset	

Your accountant will want this type of breakout of expenses for ease of explanation while he or she examines your business's profit and loss statements. Your chart of accounts will also be useful when you begin forecasting your business and developing a line-item budget.

Line-Item Budget

For those unfamiliar with the term, a "line item" is an entry in a bookkeeping ledger that represents a specific part of your business. As you can see in the example chart of accounts, each line item is assigned a number on your chart of accounts spreadsheet.

If you'd like to create your own chart of accounts (and in turn organize your own line-item breakdown), start by assigning your company bank account the number 1010.

Then, move down the ledger to income and assign each of your profit arms a 4000 series of numbers. The 4000 series includes delivered sales, commissions, retainers, refunds, etc. Also, include any loans you make to the business or loans from a bank. All must be declared as income.

After you have itemized your income, move on to the 5000–5059 series, which starts the expense side of the equation. Try to keep direct costs, such as furniture, freight, fabrics, wall coverings, and contractors, within this group. These are nonrecurring expenses and are directly related to sales income. From there, we move to the 5060 and above series for expenses related to office overhead.

Are you beginning to see how a chart of accounts is beneficial? From year to year, the same line-item number is applied to the same expenses and income, which makes it easy to see how changes (either up or down) that affect your business are happening.

Do It Yourself

It doesn't matter whether you use QuickBooks Pro or Studio IT; *you* as the designer, and not your bookkeeper, should be the one to develop your chart of accounts and line-item budgets. Your bookkeeper doesn't know what kind of reports and figures you use or where to find your profit centers. That doesn't mean you have to be secretive; you can let your accountant in on it if you'd like him or her to give you some direction. But unless you enjoy living in a world of confusion, do your charting and budgeting yourself.

In setting up your books, you should know that Hale-Williams files everything in triplicate. We keep files for the client, the firm, and the government. Each is specific in what it contains, but all have very similar information that is merely presented in a different way. If you want to be comprehensive in your reporting and protect yourself every step of the way, file in triplicate.

Profit Centers

Profit centers are directly related to the specific segments of a business, like retail, residential, commercial, product, or architectural design. Identifying a company's profit centers for recordkeeping purposes is particularly useful in running a hybrid business that operates in multiple segments (like residential firms that dabble in commercial design, or shop owners who sell product and design services). The point of the whole exercise is to see which segment or center is the most profitable part of your operation.

If you are a hybrid business owner setting up your books, here is how you do it: Like itemizing a chart of accounts, the first step is to separate out the different profit arms, or revenue streams, of your business. For instance, your profit arms might be: design fees, furniture sales, fabric sales, and lighting. Now, split up these four profit arms between the two segments of your hybrid business (like residential and commercial, or retail and design services) and find out which segment provides the largest profit.

Now, it's time to organize and analyze your profit centers. Even though, at the end of the day, your money will come back together from an accounting standpoint, organize your books so that all of your business's income doesn't flow into one big "pile." Then, analyze the data and ask yourself questions like:

- What profit center is the most profitable?
- What segment do you spend the most time working on?
- How many hours do you spend on each segment?
- Does a less-profitable segment take too much time?
- Do you work more quickly doing (for example) commercial work instead of residential work?

The goal is to be aware of what's going on at all times so, if necessary, you can take proactive steps to tweak your business model and avoid getting yourself in financial trouble.

Had we not separated out our profit centers a few years back, when we were trying to decide whether or not to keep the retail shop as part of our business, we would never have known where we were and that we weren't making money. If you're a hybrid business owner, start tracking the performance of your profit centers immediately.

Manage Your Office Time

A lot of designers have trouble managing time. Believe it or not, this is a huge area in which improvement can be made simply by building order and accountability into your routine. We have found, particularly with new entrepreneurs, that crucial resources are squandered by poorly managed projects in general.

Most first-time design entrepreneurs are not used to being their own bosses; thus, time in a workday can often slip away. Remember the old adage: "With so many moving parts, there are not enough hours." So, what is a novice to do? It's all about discipline from the get-go.

Discipline needs to translate into a designer's day-to-day operations, and the best way to ingrain it into your schedule is to stick to a routine. There is comfort and stability in repetition. It also creates respect and an understanding among staff members that there are certain times in the week for doing design work and other times for doing office work.

Start by calendaring specific days and times for bill paying, payroll, office management, and all of the other business tasks that need attention. Even if all you are doing is reviewing the work of your accountant or attorney, make a date for it in your calendar. For example, we pay bills every Tuesday, and every Friday, we review each client file so we know where the project stands. Many firms make these duties part of a weekly staff meeting.

Here are a few time management tips to consider while you build order into your burgeoning design universe:

- Stick to the rules
  - Answer e-mail, voicemail, and text messages only a few times a day, not as they come in. The point is not to be instantly available, but to have the world work around your schedule.
  - Learn when to turn off your Blackberry.
- Stick to the calendar
  - Make lists and check off items as you complete them.
  - Have a plan and stick to it.
  - If possible, don't change your schedule in reaction to a client.
  - When you are consistent in your professional routine, your clients will respect the way you do things.
- Stay focused
  - Don't allow clients to push your buttons.
  - Don't spend the day extinguishing one fire after another.
  - Don't stop what you're doing to do something else.
  - If you stop working while you are "in the zone" or "with the flow," you will lose your train of thought.
  - If you have help, don't answer every call as it comes in.

HUMAN RESOURCES

If you're planning on starting your design empire as anything larger than a "one-man band," it's a good idea to familiarize yourself with the available human resources at your disposal. Once you get rolling, you're going to find that, as with any show-business operation, it takes a village of specialists to get your projects done right.

Whether you, as the principal designer, decide to bring members of your village in-house as office managers, junior designers, design partners, or design associates remains to be seen. Certainly, all of the most successful design operations have a staff, but you're not in the same ballpark yet. While you bemoan your design infanthood, we'll introduce you to your HR options so you know what is out there.

Office Managers

For most interior designers, their first employee is an office manager. He or she runs the office, books, orders, and receiving; arranges deliveries; and attends to all other aspects of project management needed to make an office run smoothly. A good office manager need not know anything about interior design, but he or she absolutely must know a lot about business. If you decide to hire one, make sure your office manager has the business savvy to know what your goals are and how to help you achieve them.

We asked celebrity designer Mark Cutler, of Mark Cutler Design, Inc., about the positive effect a business-savvy office manager can have on a design firm. He told us about his "Anna." She is one of the best examples we know of an ideal office manager. She is so capable, in fact, that she's nearly become a partner in a very successful design firm. When we asked Mark why Anna is such a valuable asset to his business, he had this to say:

Actually, her real name is Karen Patch, but we already had a Karen working here, so she made up a name, "Anna," and goes by Anna Patch here. Anna came to the office at a time when we were just starting to blossom into an important firm. She had worked previously for another designer whom I knew well and for whom I had a huge amount of respect.

Anna came with a stronger financial background than the person who had previously held her position. Due in large part to her efforts, we have transformed the company. How? Let me count the ways:

- *I trust her management of the financial aspect of the company, so that frees me up to concentrate on developing new business and doing the creative stuff.*

- *Once she generates all of the financial reports, we go over them in detail so it is clear to me what they mean.*

- *She also instituted weekly office meetings so that the entire team goes over sales projections, time billing, etc.*

- *And, finally, we act like partners so we can be very candid and honest with each other, which really helps the business.*

Other than costing money, we find it difficult to come up with any reason why you shouldn't have an office manager, too.

Junior Designers

Hiring a junior designer is another kettle of fish. Junior designers are usually employed straight out of design school and are generally considered "junior" designers for up to two years. As a new company, you need to be certain there will be enough business to warrant the expense of taking on a junior designer. Whether they have experience or not, there's a substantial cost involved with this kind of hire.

Not only is there the employee's salary to consider, but also the overhead of taxes, unemployment, and health insurance, as well as any other perks you may offer. It all costs your firm money. The upside is that a junior designer can become one of your best allies and be great for your business. When one finally starts to mature on the job, it becomes easier to give him or her more complicated projects, which, in turn, makes it easier for you to take on larger projects and work on your firm's marketing and public relations.

The biggest downside to hiring a junior designer is the temporal nature of the relationship. If your junior designer is any good, he or she will eventually grow out of the job and venture out alone; and lonely old you will be left to start over with another junior designer. However, if you ask us, that's not all bad. Sometimes, things need to change to get better. You will also know more about exactly what you are looking for the next time around.

Design Partners

We previously touched lightly on partnerships as part of your business structure. If you remember, in chapter 6, we pegged most of you as future sole proprietors, but don't let our guesswork limit your options. Sure, being a sole proprietor is great, but it's possible that a design partnership is a better way to go. Many designers do it (and maybe you should, too) but, like a marriage, a design partnership can be a match made in heaven or in hell.

The upside is that whether it's through additional business sense, design acumen, or a larger client book, a new partner can do wonders for a small business's performance. The tricky part is managing the human angle of the partnership.

There's no way we can explain exactly how a successful partnership works. All partnerships succeed or fail for different reasons. What we *can* say is, you can't go into a partnership lightly. They are hectic. Heck, the odds of a partnership breaking up are greater than the odds of a marriage dissolving! So, needless to say, finding a worthy business partner can be a difficult endeavor. The bottom line is: All new partners should bring something positive to the table that you alone can't offer.

Maybe it's us, but designers we know who live and work together somehow tend to be more agreeable. Perhaps it's because they love each other (what a concept!), but whether it's a husband and wife team or a life partnership, spousal design partnerships just seem to get along better. What's the secret ingredient? If you ask us, they tend to have more aligned values, goals, and aspirations. As for the specific reasons for their success, they remain elusive.

Perhaps spousal partners are just comfortable with each other and, in turn, successful in that dynamic. Within our network, we know of many spousal teams who work separate sides of the same business (similar to the way we operate) and like it just fine. Sometimes, one spouse will be the office manager and do the marketing while the other is the designer. (As for how we do it, our duties tend to overlap a bit.)

The downside of spousal partnerships is that, while most couples find a way to separate business from home life, some spousal partners tend to slip into the role of two dueling workaholics who spend far too much time "talking business" when they should be enjoying life.

When it comes to non-spousal partnerships, let's just say a partnership formed by two girlfriends over a two-martini lunch has a high potential for volatility. We can flaunt this bias because it's true! While a couple of flakey, non-spousal designers may tend to jump right into a partnership, a married couple has the advantage of having spent more time getting to know the other partner.

Your partner shouldn't be your newest best friend. If you are not spouses, you should probably make sure you have a complete partnership agreement or business "prenuptial" agreement before going into business together. (We're not kidding.)

Design Associates

Design associates are different from all of the previously mentioned members of a design team in that they are independent contractors. They may appear to the outside world to be junior or partnering designers working for a firm, but they really are "associated" designers in business for themselves.

Technically, associates are not employees of a firm. They pay a monthly fee, or rent, in order to work under a successful firm's auspices or "umbrella." Unlike partners, associates have no vested or financial interest in the business and are personally responsible for their own taxes, health insurance, etc.

If this sounds like a confusing setup, it's not. Certainly, in working with a design associate, most clients don't have a clue as to how one operates. They just see a seamless, unified front office environment. But who really cares? Last time we checked, full disclosure in everything we do was not a requisite for doing business. If it were, we'd all be publicly traded commodities on the stock exchange.

There are so many different ways an associate and principal designer can scratch each other's back, we could spend a leisurely afternoon discussing all of them. Any agreement that works for you and your associate is fair game; just be creative in your modeling, and you may stumble upon an innovation that works for you.

In fact, almost a year ago, Hale-Williams Interior Design started ruminating on whether it was possible to customize the standard associate business model to make it work better for our business. We came up with something we call the "beehive associate" model, gleaned from watching people operate in the real estate and hairdressing industries. At that time, no one had applied the concept to the interior design industry, so we had to put our theory into action in order to test it. Do you want to know how the beehive associate model has worked out for us?

First, let us provide some background about how our "beehive philosophy" works. In order to come aboard, a beehive associate pays us a one-time "hive" membership fee and then subsequent monthly fees, which we call "rent." Rent covers the use of hive resources like design space, catalogues, samples, telephones, faxes, desks, filing cabinets, etc.—everything but a computer.

This is all lovely, but the real bargain for young associates is that they are able to align themselves with the Hale-Williams Interior Design hive; they are no longer wallowing in obscurity. The beehive associate is now aligned with an established, winning organization, thus giving them a leg up on their struggling counterparts who are still trying to find work or make a name for themselves.

As in going to work for Google instead of a fledgling start-up business, the benefits vary from being able to leverage the firm's reputation to land new clients to taking advantage of "sweetheart" deals the firm has with vendors and resources. Here are some more perks that young beehive associates get from this kind of alliance:

- Instant opportunity—Associates have the opportunity to create their own business under the umbrella of an established firm. They have the flexibility to either stay with the established firm or, after they establish a solid client base, walk away with their own business and client book intact.

- Instant credibility—By aligning themselves with a winning firm, design associates within the beehive model receive instant credibility. Rather than being faceless apprentices, these associates leapfrog to becoming full-fledged professional designers with all the perks.

- Instant money—With a designer logo behind them, beehive associates can instantly make more money by charging a designer price tag (i.e., higher fees).

As for what we, as principal designers, get out of the beehive alliance, you know it must be something good if we came up with the idea. Take a look at the bulleted points below and tell us what's not to like from our end:

- Monthly renter's fee—Principal designers charge beehive associates a monthly fee to rent office space, for supplies, and to leverage the firm's reputation.

- No overhead—Principal designers do not pay employee overhead for these associates, avoiding charges like commissions, benefits, worker's compensation, taxes, and any other recognized employee costs.

- No managing—Principal designers do not have to manage beehive associates by dictating hours, overseeing work, etc. Remember, they are not employees. Never forget that distinction.

- Portion of sales—Principal designers receive a portion of all associate sales by charging a small cost-plus markup on every associate purchase.

With the hive–associate relationship established, you might want to know how business is done. As you know, beehive associates purchase all of their goods through the umbrella firm at a cost-plus markup. The associate then resells the goods to his or her clients at a slightly higher price. In the end:

- The firm takes a small profit from cost-plus markup.

- The associate gets a better break on the goods, thanks to the firm's industry connections.

- The client gets an exceptional product at a reasonable price.

Everyone is happy with this setup. Our little innovation has continued to work well for us. We believe it gives us great flexibility, and flexibility is one of the Hale-Williams Interior Design keys to success in this business.

Flexibility means that business owners aren't locked into one way of doing business. If associate relationships aren't working out for any reason, the principal has the freedom to add or subtract associates when their contract comes up for review. With this flexibility, design entrepreneurs can also decide to sell, share, or change their business whenever they want.

If our beehive concept appeals to your business sense, think about how many "bees" you want buzzing around your design studio. If you are only looking to bring in one associate, consider the beehive. If you want to bring in more than one honeybee, you may want to structure your business like a cooperative (see chapter 6, "Defining Your Dream," for more on cooperatives).

In the end, it doesn't matter if you are a design entrepreneur or an independent contractor; the beehive model can work for anyone. Business owners can recruit beehive associates to work for them at any time. And in addition, you design graduates out there reading this book could even approach established design firms and propose doing business with them using the beehive model. You may be the first designer (or design associate) on the block to do it, but don't let that scare you. You're an innovator, remember? The only reason this model is not more common is because it's different and hasn't yet been heralded as the next "big thing" in the design media. But it certainly has been successful in other industries, like real estate and hairdressing.

The Associate LOA Template

If you want to write your own associate agreement, try to follow our generic example below and then see if you can customize one that suits your business:

> This letter of agreement between Robert Hale and Tom Williams of Hale-Williams Partnership and Associate, dated [insert date], is designed to highlight the points of association as agreed by both parties.
>
> - Associate will not be an employee of Hale-Williams Partnership.
> - Associate will join the partnership as an associate with no interest, either vested or financial, in the partnership.
> - Hale-Williams Partnership will not pay any commissions, benefits, workman's compensation, taxes, or any other recognized employee costs or benefits.

- Associate will operate as an individual business while renting office space from the Hale-Williams Interior Design offices in Carmel or any other offices or showrooms Hale-Williams Partnership has now or may have in the future.

- Associate will be responsible for obtaining a California resale tax certificate and a certificate for any other state in which Associate may conduct business.

- Associate will maintain own business checking account.

- Business cards will be designed by Associate and, if desired, will include the Hale-Williams Partnership logo, address, telephone number, and e-mail address.

- Associate will set own retail prices for clients who will be invoiced by Hale-Williams Partnership on Associate's behalf.

- All payments by Associate's clientele will be posted to Associate's business checking account.

- Hale-Williams Partnership will assist in all aspects of sales, promotion, ordering, client contact, and any other aspects of the business needed to succeed.

- Hale-Williams Partnership will help in creating clientele through press releases.

- Hale-Williams Partnership will work with Associate to hold a reception to announce his or her joining Hale-Williams Interior Design as an associate.

- As the association matures, Associate will be included in Hale-Williams Interior Design publicity, press releases, partnership seminars, promotions, and other events as will be mutually beneficial.

- Associate will actively participate in the selection of sales samples and will meet with representatives of the various companies with which Hale-Williams Interior Design does business.

- Associate will pay Hale-Williams Partnership monthly rent in the amount of $——. This fee includes the use of all office equipment as needed, as well as the use of samples and catalogues.

- Rent will be payable in advance on the first of each month.

- Hale-Williams Partnership will create office space with a desk, chair, telephone, DSL hook up, file cabinet, and any other item necessary for conducting business.

- If needed, Associate will supply a computer.

- Hale-Williams Partnership will prepare proposals and client bills as per Associate's requests.

- Associate will purchase all goods through Hale-Williams Partnership at cost +—— percent.

- Freight, UPS, FedEx, delivery services, and other services will be billed at cost + 10 percent.

- All purchases will be pro forma (payable in advance).

- Design fees charged by Hale-Williams Interior Design for work done by Associate will be $—— per hour to begin. Hale-Williams Interior Design will reimburse Associate at the rate of two thirds of the collected fees, irrespective of future increases in time charges. Fees will be payable on the first of the following month after collection of fees from clients.

- This agreement will be reviewed every three months for the first two years. This agreement will commence on [insert date] and may be terminated by either party with thirty days' notice.

Employee Compensation

Now that you've seen all the colors of the human resources rainbow, when you finally decide to hire an employee, you will pay them some form of compensation (as opposed to income and fees, which you charge clients). For firms looking to make the leap and grow larger, compensation will become a bigger issue.

New designers coming into the industry are expecting a lot these days. So many think they are worth $50,000 or $60,000 per year fresh out of design school. Well, guess what? They're not—not yet, anyway. Yes, employee salaries will vary depending on where they live, but rarely will a beginner start anywhere near $50,000 per year. This is because beginners have absolutely no business experience, no real design experience, and no idea how the industry or the business operates. Greenhorn designers will need a wake-up call, so prepare to remind low-level applicants that it's an entry-level position and that the salary is going to start fairly low.

Performance-Based Incentives

Today more firms are recruiting employees with precise job descriptions. This is so much the case that in many situations, young designers have to be able to consistently perform in order to secure and keep a job. Translation: no employee gets a raise just by "hanging out." That doesn't happen anymore. Employees have to prove that they are learning and moving forward within the organization, as well as helping the business earn money, before they get a bonus or salary bump. In this day and age, everyone's progress must be quantified.

Some young designers who want to be paid for their own performance may decide to go to work for a smaller design firm, where they can actually get a bigger piece of the pie based on the amount of effort they contribute. In a small firm, it's a tighter group, so one doesn't have to go through as much bureaucracy. However, in the small firms, the principal is usually doing most of the fun stuff him- or herself, so the beginning designer's role will be different.

Performance Projections

Either way a young designer goes, know that virtually every firm is attaching bonuses to performance projections these days. When you (as the business owner) are structuring your employee's contract, keep in mind that this is a unique business in which there are a lot of hand offs. A designer passes a project to a contractor, for example, who then does his thing. Then, the contractor hands the project over to a craftsman who does his part, and so on down the line. Ultimately, the project is handed over to the client, so everyone in the chain must be held accountable every step of the way. In turn, compensation must be tied to performance and execution.

Some performance projections may be based on personal goals, while others may be team-based. Surprisingly, in this system, instead of everyone taking care of him- or herself, it's often the team—and not the principal or even the individual—that makes sure the members are all performing at their optimum. Talk about efficiency! From our angle, having employees police themselves so you don't have to is not a bad way to go if you are running a large design firm.

Retirement Plans

Although there should be room for a retirement plan in your employment packages, you may not need it. A 401(k) incentive isn't as powerful as it once was. Just like in corporate America, where everyone is moving from job to job, there aren't many designers who are interested in womb-to-tomb employment anymore.

So often designers come into a firm knowing they will either move to a better job at another firm or create their own firm in a year or two. We suggest, at this early stage, that you cross this path when you come to it. We also advise you to speak to your brain trust before you establish any company retirement plan.

In Sum

Pick up a copy of *Zero Defect Hiring* by Walter Anthony Dinteman (Pfeiffer, 2003) for an in-depth discussion of the hiring process. Think long and hard about the people you invite to join your firm. They are going to be in your face every day, sharing the joys and tribulations of the business. It's all gravy when money's coming in and all are sharing in the profit, but what about the hard times? Can your new human resources strategies weather the storm? That's not for us to decide; that's for you to find out.

CHAPTER 10

BUILDING YOUR VILLAGE

Procurement, Delivery, and Installation

"A successful man is one who can lay a firm foundation with the bricks others have thrown at him."

—DAVID BRINKLEY

For all of you geniuses out there who still think every young decorator blessed with a nice studio, impressive design acumen, and effective sales mojo should be lining up a marching band for the grand opening of his or her design business, think again. There is still something missing from this equation. We haven't yet discussed how to operate your business or manage your village of partners and allies, and this chapter will address those subjects.

Ah, yes, the business side of design; that again. We're relentless, aren't we? As your mentors, we keep filling your head with business fundamentals, both because they're fundamental to your success and because we're the only designers who seem to be interested in teaching them these days! So, as we get into how to build your village and operate your office, stop designing your company logo for a moment and keep your head in the game. You're not there yet.

GETTING YOUR VILLAGE ON BOARD

Grumpy-old-men-isms aside, with your design studio set up and your business model in order, even we can see the finish line. You're not there, but you're close, so let's spend some time talking about a crucial step every designer should take before launching his or her own ship. It's called "relationship building," and you had better start doing it now if you want to hit the ground running.

Just like in Hollywood or on Capitol Hill, business relationships are the living, breathing life force of our industry. They are how all information is passed and how every deal is made. Relationships are like rainwater for the designer grapevine that, when fully nurtured, has the power to establish your business and to expand it exponentially.

So much of what we do as interior designers hinges on the working relationships we have with our design mentors, business partners, trade resources, industry colleagues, and, of course, clients; you probably want to start fostering them now. You probably don't need any more convincing, but your design network can provide many perks for your business. Your allies in this network will:

- Provide goods and services for your projects
- Refer new clients your way
- Partner with you on projects so that you both profit financially
- Serve as mentors and resources
- Expose you to media opportunities for your business

You have to have your team on board before undertaking projects so that you can make accurate estimations that will satisfy your clients on time and on budget.

Unfortunately, relationship building is not a skill they teach you in design schools. That's a shame, because other than when you are actually designing or decorating, you're going to find that your ability to leverage your network affects every move you make. We won't belabor the point, but if your formal education has failed to make you good with people, you're going to have to learn people skills on your own. If you have "people problems," take a public speaking course to get over your anxiety.

The whole point of relationship building is to make a positive, lasting impression on the world. You don't want to be remembered as a stuttering rookie, do you? Of course not. Learn to work the system and the people in the system who can help you. This is not a novel concept; it's just doing business.

POPULATING YOUR DESIGN UNIVERSE

That's right, budding entrepreneurs—it's time to conjure some internal fire and start building a design universe of your own. If you don't know where to start, allow us to clue you in to some of the Great Wonders of the Design World.

Strategic Alliances

Take it from us: You will never make it in this business unless you develop an effective means of selling yourself—not only to your clients, but also to your team of business allies. Who are they? They are the people who are going to turn your concepts into reality.

Not to state the obvious, but your allies aren't lining up to scratch your back for their health; they're doing it for theirs. That means that if an ally agrees to do you a favor (e.g., by cutting you a designer discount or by introducing you to prospective clients), you can be certain that person wants something from you in return. We designers can help our villagers by putting food on their tables through the business we give them. It is all part of the give-and-take process that goes into any great working alliance.

The objective in seeking out business allies is to form strategic alliances, which are informal partnerships between you and any professional who works in a business that can be aligned with yours. We don't mean hanging out with the guy who sells you staples at Staples; we mean forming lasting relationships with anyone who can substantially help your business. Here are some examples of a few well-oiled strategic alliances at work for a designer:

- Realtors giving designers referrals
- Architects introducing designers to clients
- Builders working with designers to produce renovations

This may sound simple, but alliances go a long way toward establishing a design career. So, as with networking, you have to get out there and meet anyone who may be of help. Avoid limiting your search to only people who can help your business operate. Any person who may be able to refer you to individuals who fit your target profile is in bounds and fair game.

Identify Your Needs

Before you start haphazardly forming alliances with every Courtney, Chad, and Ashley on the block, first sit down and identify what design products and services you are going to need to launch, and sustain, a business. Then, like a game of connect the dots, match your needs with potential allies who may not know your name yet, but soon will. Let's say you love furnishing your client spaces with antiques. You might choose to call antique dealers in town and see if they are interested in forming a strategic alliance with your firm. If you appreciate fine art, you might work on forming a strategic alliance with an art dealer or with individual artists whom you like.

This isn't rocket science; it's merely a game of connecting the stars in your design universe. You will find that some of your allies may burn brighter (and command more attention) than others, but all must coexist interdependently for your universe to prosper.

Every designer needs great service providers and source materials (be they textiles, accessories, or home furnishings), so do some research and find out what you like. Then, try to establish relationships with anyone who can fill those needs. Bust out your elevator speech and savvy sales skills to convince them of your talent and professionalism.

Some strategic alliances can be no-brainers, like aligning your firm with a dependable housepainter, upholsterer, or moving service. Why not focus attention on scooping up this kind of "low-hanging fruit" first? With those ripe relationships in the sack, move on to filling your more specialized wants and needs, like that outrageously cool "green" fabric wholesaler you've been dreaming of since your junior year.

Once you've honed in on a potential ally who is interested in doing business with your firm, arrange for a meeting so that you can sit down and talk about what each of you can do for the other's business. If, after the meeting, you come to the conclusion that both of you supply something the other demands (see Capitalism 101), see if you can come to a fair agreement. During negotiations, you both should come to a mutual understanding of the following key factors:

- What are the ground rules of the alliance?
- How does the alliance operate?
- How do both parties benefit?

Keep Agreements Informal

Although you may be compelled to jot some ideas down on paper, we suggest that you keep your alliances as informal as possible. The truth is, most relationships are informal and made with a verbal agreement as opposed to a contract or an LOA.

That's not to say you couldn't create some sort of written document to spell out exactly how the alliance works. But if you have written contracts for every relationship you have in the industry, you will limit the number of strategic alliances in which you can be involved.

Keep the agreements informal, as it's important to remain flexible when you start out. Flexibility is necessary because you may decide, after you test out an alliance, that it is not working out the way you envisioned. In such cases, you want to have the option to move on. And there is no crime in that as long as there is not a written contract.

STRATEGIC PARTNERSHIPS

Strategic partnerships are like alliances, except they are formalized with a written contract. When would a more formal relationship benefit you? Usually, when you find a sweet deal and want to ensure that you are able to take full advantage of the relationship for a sustained period of time.

Like a pro sports team that signs a young, talented athlete to a long-term contract, you want to be savvy about locking up these kinds of big-upside alliances anywhere you can. If you play your cards right, they can become an integral part of your lucrative business for years to come.

In the end, it doesn't matter who you partner with if the relationship makes sense. It all boils down to you producing the finest quality design services while making the largest profit. The most profitable relationships are the ones you want long term.

Take, for example, having a builder as a strategic partner. Hands down, this is one of the best ways to get you to the front of the bus when it comes to working with residential clients to fully realize their dreams. Partnering with a builder can be very lucrative. When you refer clients to "your" builder, you:

- Get the gratitude and back-scratching perks of a builder who will refer clients back your way

- Don't have to worry about losing business to random outside builders who affect your bottom line by convincing your clients to change your design schemes

Establishing a big-upside alliance like this can help you dictate how purchases will be made for new projects (who supplies the plumbing fixtures, flooring, special lighting, etc.) and, in general, gives you a larger piece of the pie. The earlier you define a few of these strategic alliances, the better for your business, so get out there and start talking to builders!

ESTABLISHING YOUR VILLAGE

As the saying goes, "It takes a village..." So, how do you populate your design village, and who should be asked to be a part of it? These partners and alliances are going to be the village that keeps your firm financially healthy and productive. It will be these people who have your back and know what needs to be done to insure success. Work with them.

Trade sources are another must-have in the design game. They come in the form of product representatives, furniture dealers, manufacturers, and wholesalers. Trade sources are the lifeblood of the business because manufacturers and wholesalers create and supply product.

It is important that you establish relationships with manufacturers who produce quality products and services in a timely manner. In addition, dealers and wholesalers generally represent the manufacturers and have extensive knowledge about whatever product they carry. Whether it's fabrics, furniture, or lighting, each will be well versed in the qualities and attributes of the particular product. Get to know your trade sources.

Open Accounts with Vendors

After forming a few alliances, the first step to actually doing business with your trade sources is to establish accounts with them. This is important because in order to buy anything wholesale (with a designer discount), you must have an account with that particular vendor.

In the beginning, young designers will likely be offered a pro forma account, which is an account in which every purchase is cash before delivery. We suggest that you open as many accounts as you can in the beginning while knowing that in many instances, payment in full is required simply to place the order.

You are, however, going to want to hold on to capital as long as possible in order to sustain a healthy cash flow. So it makes sense, once you have established your reputation as a reliable customer with a manufacturer, dealer, or wholesaler, to request (as much as possible) accounts where payment is made thirty days after the receipt of an invoice.

Net/30 Accounts

Net/30 accounts are active accounts in which it is agreed that the designer will pay the "net" price within thirty days. In order to obtain one of these accounts, designers are often asked to agree to be personally responsible should the bill not be paid. It also usually involves filling out a credit application, in which the designer will be asked about other open accounts, bank accounts, and some personal information.

This may sound scary to beginners, but it is essentially a good business practice because it buys you time and sometimes even allows for the delivery of goods and the client's payment of the balance to occur before you as the designer have to pay the vendor. Remember, the most important part of commercial success is the ability to deftly manage your cash flow. By not having to pay up front, your company has the use of the money for at least thirty additional days, if not longer. That is good business.

Buying Wholesale

Buying products at wholesale should not be confused with buying products at a designer discount. Wholesale is a price quoted from the vendor to the designer that is understood to be the lowest the vendor will go to move the item. Wholesale is usually reserved for designers who are known to the vendor and who have open net/30 accounts.

Quoted wholesale prices are technically net prices that have been fixed by the vendor because the designer is a repeat client. The greatest benefit of wholesale is that it allows a better markup on the sale of the item for the designer and, of course, a better bottom line.

Designer Discounts

Designer discounts are not the norm. They are only made from time to time at certain retail establishments, usually as a courtesy. That means that like everything we do in business, you have to work all the angles to improve your bottom line. Designer discounts have nothing to do with how showrooms and "to the trade" establishments do business, even though inexperienced decorators often refer to trade prices as a designer discount.

Showrooms often price items at a "retail" price and then reduce that price by 40 percent for designers. This price could also be referred to as the showroom net price. It is not a wholesale price. The showroom pays the wholesale price to the manufacturer, then marks the product up to the designer. It would be wonderful if all designers could buy everything wholesale, but that, too, is not the norm. Many times, there are minimum purchase requirements that designers can't always meet. So, showroom owners, who buy in larger quantities and maintain floor samples, will always charge a small premium for the service they offer to designers.

Discount Disclosure

Who is "in" on a discount once it has been established? It depends on how your letter of agreement or contract has been constructed. If you are selling all items at "presented price," there is no need for anyone but you to know what the wholesale price is on any item. If, on the other hand, you are working on a "cost-plus" contract, you will need to be able to produce the invoice should the client inquire.

On your client invoice, you will usually reference the net price to show the markup you charged to arrive at the retail price. Yes, we said retail. If you are selling anything at a profit, you are selling retail. Either way you choose to sell items, make sure you are completely aware of what they will cost you and what your markup will be.

It isn't unscrupulous for the designer to pocket the designer discount from a retail establishment. In fact, most designer discounts are indeed kept by the designer, especially if that was the agreement between the client and the designer in the beginning. Why is this cool with clients? Because keeping the small commission really is the only way the designer can make any money on the item if he or she isn't charging time for this particular service.

Depending on the crowd you run with, you may come across some designers of (dare we say it?) questionable moral fiber who get a discount and tell their clients they are passing the savings on to them, only to keep the entire amount for themselves.

Don't be a designer Enron; you know what happened to them. If you try to pull a fast one, and you and your client have already agreed to use transparent pricing for the purchase, you could have an extremely unhappy client on your hands. Don't risk your reputation and your business for a few under-the-table dollars. It's just not worth it.

Product Representatives

Product representatives (reps) can be a small-market designer's best friends. If you fit the profile, they are your pipeline to the industry, your eyes and ears that keep you informed about the latest products, services, and industry trends. Reps are usually found traveling on the road, where they spend the bulk of their time visiting interior designers who can't get to the design centers in major metropolitan areas.

The rep, like the dealer, has a comprehensive knowledge of his or her product and will usually bring the very latest examples of what he or she has to sell. Reps are also the first point of contact for those design firms with large libraries that are located far from design centers. Regardless of where you live, do yourself a favor and cozy up to product reps who represent the products and services you love best. They will work with you as a designer to:

- Ask for and get volume discounts
- Resolve disputes over shipping and damage charges
- Be your voice to the wholesaler or manufacturer

Craftsmen

Craftsmen are experts skilled at producing and installing custom-made products, furniture, and accessories. They include people who install wall coverings, build custom cabinetry, and paint commercial and/or residential spaces.

Craftsmen are important because they create the truly "bespoke," or handmade, products that give luxury residential and commercial design their quality look. In seeking out this kind of alliance, try to make sure your craftsmen know how to run a business. You must be confident that they will produce items in a timely manner. The fact is, your reputation with your clients and in the industry depends on how they perform. No matter how much you like someone on a personal level, never align yourself with a shoddily run outfit. It will only lead to heartache in the end.

At times, as a designer, you might have to act as a business consultant for some of your craftsmen, securing new jobs, speaking with clients for them, and so forth. Don't be afraid to promote your craftsmen; remember that if you scratch their backs, they just might scratch yours in return. Once you start to collect a nice array of dependable craftsmen who produce great work, you're going to feel much more prepared to open your doors and recruit clients.

Contractors

Electricians, flooring specialists, tile installers, carpet installers, plumbers, and contractors can all be the bane of a designer's existence. Many are very professional and get the job done in a timely manner; some, however, are not. Be sure you understand your needs before working with a contractor, because if you haven't clearly defined the parameters of your working relationship, miscommunication is inevitable. To combat any miscommunications, simply make sure your contractors understand how you operate as a firm and what your expectations are when it comes to timelines and the finished product.

As for how much control you want to give up on a project, it's up to you. We personally never turn over control of our projects, but manage our contractors, instead. This is not a bad way to go, if you ask us; but don't take our word for it. Use your own judgment to decide which way works best for your business.

Bank Advisors

Remember: just because your banking advisor is always smiling doesn't mean he or she has your best interests in mind. Your banker is not your accountant, so tread lightly when you source one. This is America, where most banks are commercial organizations that are in it for the profit. Bankers are selling a product just as designers sell product, so read all the small print twice and do not depend on the banker to lead you to the best loan or line of credit for your company. Get a second opinion from your accountant. That's why you hired one, right?

Credit Advisors

We won't go into great detail here about credit advisors, as they should be discussed with your brain trust (and specifically your CPA). We can tell, however, that most reputable credit advisors doing business these days will try to direct you to the best loan or line of credit products on the market. Take into consideration that these people also oftentimes charge some sort of fee, whether in the form of a flat-out payment or in the form of "points" within the loan. Make sure fine print factors like fees are disclosed during negotiation.

Insurance Advisors

Most design entrepreneurs work with a number of insurance underwriters in forming their businesses. If you do your research, you shouldn't have much trouble finding underwriters who will sell you the best product available, whether it's automobile, liability, or business insurance.

The last thing you want is to be held liable for any kind of damage without being properly insured. A catastrophic accident can ruin a small business, so meet with your insurance advisor and go over your options.

Insurance Options

Bonding is the act of taking out a policy with an insurance company, so that if you commit a crime while providing a service (and are convicted), the bonding company will pay the client back for you. Bonding protects your business because it allows you to pay the insurance company back over a period of time, plus interest. Here are a few other insurance options commonly used by professional designers:

- Renters insurance—Most property owners require a liability policy in case of fire, damage, flood, pestilence, etc.

- In addition to renters insurance and bonding, some wealthy clients will require you to be insured in case your firm damages their home or property during installations.

- Professional liability insurance—This insurance covers liability for claims resulting from the commission or omission of professional acts.

- Group medical—This policy covers health insurance for your firm.

Technical Advisors

We're not sure about you, but we have information technology (IT) advisors for the technology in our office. You hotshots may be able to handle your electronics by yourself, but if you are like most designers (i.e., technologically challenged), you may want to recruit one. We call in our Geek Squad when things happen and we have no idea how to correct them. We also use them for Web hosting and managing our Web site to ensure that we are always near the top of search engine results.

Use the Golden Rule

Now that you know more about some of the key players in your design universe, when it comes to managing your cast, try to use the golden rule in every interaction. You still remember that old chestnut, don't you? Do unto others as you would have them do unto you.

The modern design translation of this timeless adage is simple: be positive, professional, clear, and consistent at all times when dealing with your villagers, and the world will be a better place. Make a sustained effort to keep "your team" happy. After all, that's what they are: your team.

Always, and we mean always, praise good work when the job is done to your specification. The payoff is that when the time comes to talk about a project that might not be up to your standards, it will be easier to make the adjustment. Each party will know the other has his or her respect and is not, in any way, trying to take advantage.

Remember, both sides must respect and appreciate the work of the other, or the alliance is off. A professional designer will *never* yell, scream, become hysterical, or in any way try to demean or belittle the people with whom he or she works. At the same time, a professional will not tolerate that type of behavior from vendors or associates. Be sure that your team has bought into this philosophy of respect, or you will face problems and possible mutiny down the road. Not only will this mutual respect make your working relationships easier, but fostering mutual respect also makes your sales job to your clients that much simpler. Respecting your allies gives you confidence that you can produce what you say you will. Confidence in every cog in the process makes it easier for you to sell.

EXPANDING YOUR NETWORK

Okay, so we've talked a lot about tactical allies so far. Now, how about expanding your brain trust to include other designers who can serve as resources and mentors? It sounds like a good idea, but finding ones you can trust is the hard part.

So, often in this dog-eat-designer-dog world, designers simply will not share business practices with other local designers. They are too competitive to want to share any trade secrets with the enemy. In addition, many designers are also very jealous and territorial about what they perceive as their "turf."

Long-Distance Designers

So, what's a lonely designer to do? You might want to befriend designers from other parts of the country. Just as familiarity breeds contempt, a lack thereof can do wonders for a professional relationship. Once you strike up a relationship with a long-distance designer, you'll find that all of the competitive juices usually go away.

Most of these virtual colleagues will be very honest with you about how they do business and offer up some tricks of the trade that could come in very useful in your neck of the woods. A good way to meet designers from other parts of the world is to join the right professional design group or attend at least one major design conference a year.

Join the Right Professional Group

As you know, we're not huge fans of the traditional professional design groups. Unfortunately, our profession is populated with many untalented, insecure, and often downright mean people. That said, we believe it is vital to keep in contact with other designers, so we became members of a national conference and networking group called Designing Profits, Inc.

We believe that Designing Profits, Inc., is one of the most professional business groups—not just of interior design business groups, but the best business group, bar none—in existence today. We wouldn't be writing this book if we were not members. (Frankly, we wouldn't be doing a lot of things we do in business had we not joined.)

It all started with David Shepherd, the Alan Greenspan of the design industry. An author, professor, and business practices guru, David put together a conference series back in 2002 called the Business of Design Conference, produced by his company, Designing Profits, Inc. The conference and its select networking community, called BPN—Best Practices Network—keeps giving back. Our industry is so diverse, smaller professional groups like this give designers the chance to connect with good people who are having similar experiences. The ability to share information with other BPN designers has been priceless to our firm.

After joining, we were inspired to change the way we run our business, from adjusting our billing practices, to raising fees, to focusing our marketing efforts. The strength of the organization is that members are really willing to open up and discuss how they do business. Whether it's because they come from other parts of the country or because the BPN attracts people who want to share, the bottom line is that we know it works.

Attend Design Conferences

We started attending conferences very early in our careers and learned so much that other than the cost, we cannot think of any reason why a young designer shouldn't follow suit. For a good example of how this practice benefited us when we were just starting out, let's go back to one of the first conferences either of us ever attended.

When I (Tom) was still a neophyte living on the East Coast, the Philadelphia Design Center sponsored a yearly market conference that attracted designers from all over. Even as a young whip, I jumped at the chance to attend and meet other designers who could help me develop my chops. It turned out to be a deft move, because in addition to the networking I accomplished with business allies at the conference, I also took advantage of the fact that most major design conferences also hold seminars and presentations. Make it a point to attend at least one conference a year, and you will get a great amount of exposure to what is happening in the industry and in the field, regardless of which conference you choose.

For over ten years, we were also members of the International Furnishings and Design Association. We both served locally as board members, and one of us (Tom) served on the national board of directors for three years. This group, created in the 1940s as the Women's Home Fashion League, is comprised of professionals (both men and women now) and industry partners. All members have equal status, and many of the local organizations are very active and strong. Over the years, we've been able to stay in touch with those designers we met years ago. To this day, they still love to talk to us about their business, and we to them.

We gleaned much of our business acumen by forming alliances with other designers. You can, too, if you continue to take action, meet people, and think of creative ways to expand your universe.

PURCHASING

With a resource file full of contact information and a head full of new ideas, you're more prepared now than ever to really do business. Talk about empowerment! Now, do you think you're ready to take on the nitty-gritty tactical maneuvers that go into operating a design studio like procurement, delivery, installation, and billing? You thought your office was a mess before, but just wait—we're only getting warmed up.

In this limited space, we can't get into a comprehensive discussion on purchasing. We could talk your ear off, but (as we've said before) there are a lot of textbooks out there that will give you all of the materials you need for purchasing goods. If you want a book of templates for purchasing, invoicing, etc., we suggest you buy Mary Knacksted's *The Interior Design Business Handbook* (Wiley, 2001) or the aforementioned *Business and Legal Forms for Interior Designers*. We're not interested in recreating the wheel on these pages, but what we *are* interested in is providing you with a road map that explains how it works. So, let's go shopping, shall we?

Sourcing Products

Sourcing products is kind of like hunting for Easter eggs. You never know what you're going to find and you may, at times, grow fussy in your search. Nevertheless, you must press on through rain, sleet, snow, or dark of night. Your goal is to find that special something your client will not be able to live without each and every time.

Some designers simply have a nose for sourcing the perfect products, while others struggle mightily to find what they need. We can't give you a reason or a blueprint for how to do it in your world. Sourcing really is another one of those intangible skills that you either have or you don't. That said, here are a few tips:

- Lean on your network of allies and mentors.
- Scour the Internet; it's a great resource. Some designers procure everything off the Web.
- Stay current by reading "shelter" magazines and trade publications.
- Visit your favorite design centers and retail establishments often. Put on your detective hat and ask around.
- Follow through with every lead.
- Test-drive products yourself.

Customize It

If all else fails, do what we do: find a business ally who can custom-make products that meet your client's exact specifications. It may cost more, but it's something every luxury designer must be able to execute to fulfill his or her client's needs.

You may be surprised to find how cost-efficient some custom-made products can be. Even if you're targeting a middle-class clientele, don't be afraid to at least explore the possibility of aligning yourself with custom craftsmen. In our experience, we have found some who are so hungry for regular work that they will cut you a nice deal as a sign of good faith.

Tear Sheets

Every young designer should become familiar with tear sheets, which are one-page itemized descriptions (with photos) of an individual product, fabric, accessory, or piece of furniture. Vendors create tear sheets as mini-advertisements for products, while interior designers use them in proposing products to clients and as a general reference point.

Client Proposals

After you source the perfect products, it's time to show them off to your client. While some clients may be willing and able to accompany the designer to view the sourced items at a local retail shop or design center, oftentimes, a designer will have to go to the client to present recommendations. Before your recommendation meeting, you should create a client proposal for the goods or services involved and include the tear sheet. If you recall from our pricing discussion, we generally break up each individual piece we sell as an individual proposal.

So, for us, a drapery is a proposal, a sofa is a proposal, two chairs are a proposal, one cocktail table is a proposal, and two side tables are a proposal. Some designers have even been known to incorporate new pieces of furniture, fabric, etc. into their clients' floor plans to show them how the new items will look in their home.

Since every client these days wants lots of options when it comes to buying something of value, most designers bring along a Plan A to a Plan E to improve the chances that the client will like what he or she is being offered. That means that if your client wants to furnish his study with, say, a club chair, you may source several chairs and then bring the tear sheets to the client to see if any of them appeals to him or her.

Client and Vendor Deposits

After the written proposal is prepared and presented and the client has signed off on the purchase, wait to receive the approved proposal from the client. It must be signed and dated. Along with the written approval, designers always request some form of deposit for an order. Since vendors request a deposit from designers, why shouldn't we request a deposit from our clients?

Remember, it's all about managing your cash flow, so the quicker you get your client's money in your hot little hands, the quicker it begins to work for you. If you are just starting out, odds are you'll be working with limited capital (i.e., flying by the seat of your pants), at least for your first projects, so you will likely use your client deposits to pay vendor deposits.

As for what percentage of the purchase you should demand up front, it varies throughout the industry. We charge 70 percent to place the order, with the 30-percent balance due before receipt or installation of goods. If that sounds a tad steep, that's because it probably is for beginners. To be in line with your industry peers, consider a 50-percent deposit in the beginning. For those designers with a very limited cash flow, you may have to charge more.

Purchase Orders

In every sale, the designer must create a purchase order. Whether for fabric, trim, textiles, or furniture, a purchase order is your instruction to the vendor to proceed with the implementation of an order. Take note that in today's marketplace, many vendors will not proceed without a written order. We suggest that you make three copies of every purchase and distribute them in this fashion:

- The first copy goes to the vendor.

- The second copy goes with the proposal for the client file.

- The third copy goes into the on-order file.

Once you have supplied your vendor with a deposit, if required, for the item, he or she then processes the order.

The Waiting Game

With the order processed, now it's on to a waiting game where some impatient clients have been known to cause a stink. It may take up to six months to receive a custom-made Italian bed that you've purchased. Quality goods take time to be handcrafted, so naturally, some clients tend to get antsy, especially when they paid a 70-percent deposit six months ago and the bed still hasn't arrived.

It would be an understatement to say that many clients are not used to waiting so long for a product to arrive. But this is reality in the bespoken designer universe, so be prepared to field nervous or angry calls from clients whose lives depend on knowing the exact date when their order will arrive.

To quell their fears, it is imperative that you know where each order is on the track to completion. It's also mandatory to know what money is owed and when. In tracking orders, a system of purchase-order numbering is essential. We suggest that you:

- Use QuickBooks Pro, Studio IT, or other management software to track client and vendor deposits

- Create an alphabetical filing system for tracking orders

- File all your open purchase orders by vendor name

Order Files, Client Files, and Vendor Files

While you're waiting on your deliveries, it's time to do some paperwork. It's not always the most fun, but it's exactly what you must do to stay on top of your orders.

Start by creating an order file for each purchase. Order files capture all the necessary documents for an individual order. Most designers divide their order files by vendor. In addition, you should store all tear sheets in the appropriate job book or client file for future reference. Some designers will even file tear sheets in a separate vendor file if needed.

It may be useful to know that Studio IT project management software has a memo feature in which you can include notes on purchase orders and keep track of all conversations. Trust us: You positively must keep track of conversations you have regarding every order. And don't slack off on your reporting. We print out e-mails all the time and keep them with individual client folders. The reason we file all the details is to avoid getting into any games of "he said, she said" with vendors. Unnecessary conflict will only delay receipt of goods and cause you endless misery.

THINKING OUTSIDE THE BOX

Now that you understand the scope of the paperwork that goes into procurement, at some point, you need to decide who is going to do all this work. Three potential options are:

- Doing all the paperwork, follow-up, and tracking yourself
- Hiring a full- or part-time "paper pusher"
- Outsourcing the work

If you choose to outsource, working with a purchasing service might be the answer to the future staffing problem many of you will have early in your careers. There are plenty of good reasons to use such a service, especially if you work from home:

- The outside service supplies all needed credit.
- The service lets designers pay easily by credit card or check.
- All tracking and follow-up is handled by the service.
- Until the item is delivered, everything is handled by the service.
- Hiring a service isn't nearly as expensive as hiring full-time staff.

Sure, these groups charge, but that's what service is all about, right? That and being able to track all your orders and make sure they are delivered in a timely matter is a valuable tool. Does this sound like a good deal to you? Well, here are the downsides:

- It costs money.
- Like a game of "telephone," essential information can get lost in the translation, thereby confusing vendors and mucking up orders.
- Timing can be an issue if the purchasing group and the designer are located in different time zones.
- Due to the customization craze, some designers have to be in constant communication with certain vendors about specifics. A conduit would not make sense for their business.

As your firm grows larger, it may be more profitable to bring this type of management in-house, but while you are young and just starting out, we'd go for the purchasing service. By the time your business is ready to grow, you will have a much better idea of how you want the process to flow within the firm and won't need the outside resource. Any way you choose to go out of the gate, purchasing groups are a service that, we believe, will help a lot of young designers get through the first few years of running a small business.

RECEIVING, INVOICING, AND BILLING

A designer's paper trail doesn't end when the client purchases finally start trickling in. Your engine has to keep rolling at all times. There is so much paperwork involved in every client order that if a designer drops a ball (by forgetting to submit an invoice on time, for example), the whole juggling act gets thrown out of whack. Savvy designers stay on top of every client transaction.

We know that accounting for everything may appear tedious or confusing to the beginners who have never before set foot inside an office, but you will adjust. We all do. Now let's keep walking you through the accounting process so that you continue getting the hang of it.

You probably know that, after finally receiving a shipment of your purchases, you should not immediately rush to your client in a rented U-Haul to deliver the goods. That's not exactly how it's done in the big leagues. There is still homework to be done. Please duly note the following tips before you start delivering anything.

Proof the Bill

Upon receipt of goods, the first thing smart designers do is put all of the written purchase orders back together in order to proof the bill. You must be sure that:

- You were charged the prices quoted to you
- You received all the ordered goods
- Charges (like shipping and handling) were not snuck into the final bill unless they were agreed upon when the order was placed

If you can check off the above three bullets, move on to updating your records. All pending orders should be moved from the tracking file to the received file. You can write the received date on the purchase order or note it in your computer's tracking system (or both). Either way, when you're ready to bill the client, purchase orders are removed from the received file and attached to the in-office copy of a client invoice.

Client Invoicing

A client invoice is a written document that contains a list of goods "sent" or services "provided" with a statement of the deposit paid and amount due. Since no one in this industry (clients included) pays a bill without a written invoice, designers need to put together a hard-copy billing package that stays in the client file and includes one or all of the following documents:

- The client proposal
- The product proposal
- The purchasing invoice
- The hourly time invoice

After you have received the paid invoice, the document will eventually find its way into the paid invoice file.

Billing for Time

If you include an hourly rate in your pricing structure, you need to know how to bill for time. An hourly time invoice is slightly different than a purchasing invoice in that it requests payment for the hours a designer has put into a project. Hourly billing usually occurs after the client has used all of his or her designer retainer.

Be thoughtful but diligent when calculating your hours. We have found that the most common client conflicts seem to occur around the issues of pricing and time charges. This is because these issues deal with money, and due to bad buzz, some clients perceive interior designers as a pack of unscrupulous charlatans.

In the eyes of many skeptical clients, we are guilty until proven innocent, so always prepare for cross-examination. Know that however you go about hourly billing, if you're like most designers, you will probably get some unsolicited "feedback" at some point in your career.

Have Defined Systems for Billing

The best way to prove to clients that you are inherently ethical is to run a tight ship. In this case, having defined systems for time sheets is the beginning. Really spell it out for them before the project begins. That way, early on, the designer has established a routine that will instill trust in the client. And any mistakes that are made will hopefully be caught as they happen rather than when the client sees the invoice.

Additional steps toward defining your billing system include:

- Maintaining up-to-date billings and invoices
- Making sure proper time is kept on each client job
- Making sure you bill within the time period stipulated in the contract

If that means checking each invoice twice and then having someone else check it, that's okay. Never send out a billing invoice with an error in calculation or amount. It is unforgivable, and believe us, the client won't forget.

Show Clients the Way

Gioi Tran of Applegate Tran Interiors had some interesting things to say about the challenge of hourly billing in chapter 3. He said, "All designers have a method to their madness; but unless you're a savvy salesperson and an excellent communicator, your clients will just see the madness and miss the method. It's up to you to show them the way."

In the end, some clients will haggle while others will pay with a smile. In dealing with a strong opinion, thank the client for his or her feedback, listen, and nod with a smile, then charge the rate you want to charge, stand by your convictions, and don't back down.

Once you mail off the client invoice (and your hourly invoice), it's time to wait for your client to send you a check for the remainder of the balance before delivery. Rather than twiddle your thumbs, how about some more paperwork?

Pay Your Vendors on Time

It is important to pay your vendor invoices promptly. Your vendors are your partners—remember? They expect to be paid on time just as you do. Prompt payment also helps if, at some point, you need extra time to pay an invoice. Your stellar track record will give you a lot of brownie points with vendors, making them far more likely to listen to you if you ever need to make a case for a longer billing period.

Sales Tax

Sales tax must be paid for almost every transaction in the design industry. There are a few things that are tax exempt in this world (for example, time charges are not taxable in our area), but most of what we designers sell is not exempt.

That means that unless you live in a sales tax–exempt state, like Alaska, Montana, New Hampshire, or Delaware, you need to know how to record, calculate, and, of course, pay the government what you rightfully owe.

The upside is that most states rely on the honesty of a business to collect, report, and pay sales tax once the goods have been received. In California, sales tax is payable on a monthly basis, but laws vary from state, county, and municipality. Listen to your accountant when it comes to setting aside money for all of your business taxes.

Paying taxes may not sound glamorous, but it is a mandatory requirement in this country. In fact, if you don't pay "the man," the tax authority can shut your business down so fast it will make your finely coiffed head swim. To avoid such a calamity, here are a few more tax tips to take with you from our little accounting boot camp:

- Hold a reserve—Hold money you collect for taxes so you have it on hand to file your monthly report.

- Never·negotiate sales tax—Never tell a client you will deduct sales tax as a way to close the deal. Sales tax is not a part of the negotiation. If you want to take something off, take it off the item. That will reduce the sales tax.

- Pay sales tax once a month—The importance of paying on a regular basis is part of most state tax codes. Sales tax actually generates a big chunk of revenue for most areas, so most tax collectors are very strict about payment.

- Get electronic reporting—Find out if you live in a state that allows for electronic tax reporting.

- Find out if you qualify for quarterly payments—Some businesses are allowed to pay quarterly sales tax, so ask your accountant if your business qualifies.

- Create a tax storage file—Store a copy of each paid invoice in a tax storage file for your annual taxes.

DELIVERY AND INSTALLATION

Let us imagine that your client has finally sent you the check for the remainder of the balance and you are ready to handle a delivery to the client's home. With your client invoice paid, the next step is to call in your moving team to deliver the items.

To a young designer who is still establishing his or her reputation, there is nothing more valuable than an excellent delivery firm and installation group. The flipside to that pancake is that there is nothing more harmful than aligning your firm with an incompetent outfit that breaks or damages goods in transit. You must hire pros if you want to look like a pro.

We use a professional moving company that has a specific area of their warehouse dedicated to design clients. Every item is inspected upon arrival, then rewrapped and stored in their warehouse until the client delivery. When the time comes, our movers arrive on time and in uniform.

These movers wear booties while they are in a client home and spread clean moving pads throughout the house during delivery. Certainly, it costs more, but not much more—only about 25 percent. If you ask us, it's worth every penny for the ease of installation and comfort of mind. Sometimes saving a few bucks just isn't worth the grief of dirty trucks and nasty delivery people. If you want to look like a professional, hire one.

If you choose to be a luxury designer, in particular, you must respect the fact that you are responsible for valuable goods. That means that if something goes wrong and you haven't used a professional service, your reputation is on the line.

Installations

Some design products actually require that you hire a specialist to install them. In installing custom-made draperies, flooring, and art, as well as some custom-made furniture and appliances, always try to work with the same installation specialists to improve your chances of getting a consistent customer experience.

For example, when we do drapery installations, we use a professional who works with the drapery workroom and also does the check measure for the creation of the product. That way, there is only one place to go if something isn't just right. Again, these people are worth every penny to insure a perfect installation at the time of delivery.

If you walk away from our design symposium with one lesson, let it be this: do not install anything yourself. Many designers young and old have made the mistake of trying to do it themselves and thereby have royally screwed up what could have been a simple installation of a valuable piece of furniture.

Don't be a sucker. Just because you ordered a Mercedes doesn't mean you know how to install the brake pads. Yet, some designers still think they do. Oh, we suppose some designers simply lose their good judgment when they are under stress and trying to save money. Or perhaps they assume they can whip out an installation on their own to save the day when the installation people they called don't show up.

Think before you leap. What if you were to damage the piece? Are you insured? The deliverymen certainly are, but you probably are not, so be wise. Do not make a rookie mistake by getting thrown out at home base.

CYA or Prepare to Pay

We will confess to having pulled a few doozies in our career, learning the hard way on several occasions that it takes a professional to install something correctly. We won't tell you about any of those (having wiped them from our memory banks), but we will warn you that even professional movers make mistakes from time to time.

Probably the most absurd installation experience we've had in our career was the time our framer installed a rather large piece of art over a mantle in the home of one of our clients, Cal Ripken, Jr., only to have it come crashing down on top of one of his Most Valuable Player trophies. (Oops. Is that trophy supposed to be in so many pieces?)

Well, it happened. We designed the beautiful home of Cal and his wife, Kelly, in Baltimore back when we were living on the East Coast. The only snafu in the project came during that particular installation. How we cringed when it all came crashing down within minutes of the installation. Both the artwork and the mantle were slightly damaged along with the trophy. The framer immediately stepped up to the plate (we just couldn't resist) and repaired everything at his expense. The Ripkens understood, and we were all able to laugh about it. And (thank goodness!) Major League Baseball was able to send Ripken another MVP trophy. There's no way we could have replaced that!

Wrapping Your Head Around It

Well, folks, that's procurement, delivery, and installation in a nutshell. Now, it's up to you to learn how to manage your cash flow, clients, resources, and time (more on that in the next chapter).

When it comes to accounting for everything, don't let it freak you out. The best thing you can do at the outset of your career is make sure you have systems in place so you know where everything is. That really is the key. We know that this is all easier said than done, but don't forget that you have a network of business allies to help, and you're getting wiser by the day. You also have an accountant and tools like Studio IT, which allow you to easily keep good records of proposals, deposits, and balances due.

Every CYA business practice you absorb into your consciousness brings you a little closer to becoming the design entrepreneur you were born to be. We'll leave you with some additional "commandments" that will help you be an effective office manager:

- Thou shall treat resources as partners in your business.
- Thou shall have a written purchase order for every client order.
- Thou shall take a deposit for every client order.
- Thou shall pay bills by invoice only.
- Thou shall create purchase orders for all goods from vendors.
- Thou shall track and bill for hourly fees.
- Thou shall have open net/30 accounts with vendors.
- Thou shall take a retainer (design fee) for all projects.
- Thou shall live by a yearly budget.
- Thou shall have a balanced business checking account.
- Thou shall pay all bills and invoices in a timely manner.
- Thou shall never install something thyself.
- Thou shall never do favors.

CHAPTER 11

CLIENT MANAGEMENT

Game-Planning Your Design Business

"Never get in the way of your client; your job is to create a home that is a portrait of [him or her], not a vehicle for your ego...."

—MARK CUTLER

Armed with a newfound sense of how the procurement process works (from orders, to billing, to installations), we plan to spend some time in our final chapter discussing one of the biggest factors that goes into determining whether a young talent blossoms into a top-shelf designer: the ability to deftly manage clients.

CLIENT MANAGEMENT

It doesn't matter if you are the most charming person; every young entrepreneur needs to develop excellent client management skills in order to maintain a healthy client base. As you now know, making a living as an interior designer is a tough racket. Contrary to what you may see on television, most clients are actually much harder to deal with in the real world, especially when they work with a designer who is just starting out.

While you beginners brace for the inevitable, know that with a healthy regimen of business practices built into your operation, most client issues can be avoided. All you have to do is add a few extra steps to your routine.

The first step in effectively managing clients is establishing control over the execution of the project. It may sound rudimentary, but you will be surprised at how many clients will challenge your authority. After they hire you for a project, far too many modern clients will try to manage, or at least passive-aggressively micro manage, "the show" themselves if you let them. Do not let them. Never let a client dictate how much you charge for time or how much is taken for deposits. It is up to the design firm.

One reason why so many modern clients hire young, inexperienced designers is so they can better control them. If you haven't gathered, this is not the way it works with professionals, but some young decorators allow it to happen. We advise you not to make the same mistake; however, if you're into horror and want to play by someone else's rules, go ahead. Don't say we didn't warn you.

One Chef in the Kitchen

If you're like us, you require complete control over a project or you're not doing it. Control is important because it gives you confidence, which allows you to perform at a high level. When you are in control, you are in command. You know every source to tap and every button to push to realize your client's vision. You're an unstoppable design machine, and that feels good.

Though we may be overdramatizing our role just a bit, other benefits of controlling a project are increased knowledge (like knowing exactly when deposits have been paid and when balances are due) and power (i.e., you're the only cook in the kitchen when you work with contractors and vendors). Both are good to have on your side.

Confidence, knowledge, and power are what every designer needs to succeed. In order to have them, you must set ground rules with clients. At the beginning of a project, create an outline that stipulates your business rules and includes a project timeline for what you're going to be doing day to day and week to week. Let your clients know it's okay to collaborate with you in conceptualizing designs and selecting furniture, textiles, accessories, etc. But it's not okay for them to actively participate any further than that.

Project Timeline

At no point should you ever approve of clients contacting vendors, tracking orders, receiving shipments, or installing anything. This is what we call crossing the line. The key to avoiding any confusion is to be straight with your clients. Tell them when they can participate and tell them graciously when they need to back off.

Literally note on your project timeline that from this day forward, you (the designer) will take control, making sure that selections happen in a timely manner and that goods are ordered, delivered, and installed properly. We might appear insensitive, but if you ask us, it really doesn't matter how clients would like to do business. It's up to the design firm to establish business practices.

Waiting Game Woes

After you have completed the conceptual and selection stages, all the client has to do is sit back, pay the invoices, and wait...and wait...and wait. And therein lies the rub. As we mentioned in the previous chapter, this "twilight zone" time can get tedious for everyone. Clients hate to pay invoices and wait for months to receive a custom-made piece of furniture, so they complain, they fuss, and they call. What they need from you is order to soothe their furrowed brows. Give it to them from the beginning, and then some.

Stand by your system and feel free to say, "This is the way I do business; it is not negotiable." The client then understands who is in charge of the management of the project and who is in charge of making the business decisions. And, for heaven's sake, do not cave when a client complains, because many will. If you stick to your guns, they will respect you for professionally laying out the process in the beginning, then seamlessly executing the project plan. Can you see we're not talking about being flashy here? We're preaching consistency. Communication and consistency are the two magic bullets to building trust with clients.

Stage two in establishing control is making sure you adhere to all of your own business rules at all times. At this point, it should not be a newsflash that many flighty designers have problems with consistency. It is not uncommon to see a designer establish a fabulous set of ground rules and then not live up to them.

Once a client has bought into your system, don't screw it up by dropping the ball! We can't stress how important it is to be consistent in all of your business dealings. If you are as sharp as a tack at all times, the client gets used to the fact that you are a perfectly professional designer who is selling product and time, and stops questioning your every move.

As a designer, consistency in everyday actions translates to:

- Doing everything you say you're going to do with a smile
- Getting in the good graces of your clients and staying there
- Selling product and never changing the way you do it
- Handling tasks like hourly billing in a professional, timely manner

At some point, you may have to ask for an additional design fee. Don't hesitate to do it! Don't let clients drive how you do business. Make sure you tell them what needs to be done.

Client Communication Guide

In many cases, designers also have to teach clients rules of etiquette when it comes to communication. Set up your guidelines early. They don't have

to be included in your LOA; you can always write a separate communications guide that states how you will communicate with clients and
manage projects. We realize that for the hungry, the concepts of "communication guides" and "client control" are hard to get a handle on. You're
young and just want to fly by the seat of your pants. It has worked so far
in life, so why change now?

The answer is all about being true to your business philosophy and
the way you want to run your office. If you don't lay everything out early,
something will come back to bite you—be sure of it. You don't necessarily
have to compose a written page of rules, but you do have to be clear with
clients from the beginning.

Here are a few guidelines to consider that work for many designers:

- Guard your privacy—Do not give out your private cell phone
  number. Some clients feel they have bought you, so don't give
  them the chance to cross the line.

- No 24/7 live contact—A client does not have the right to
  contact you live 24/7. You're not required to instantly answer text
  messages or voicemails unless it is a critical situation. Nothing we
  do is life-threatening, so tell your clients to get over it.

- Twenty-four-hour rule—Let clients know you are always available
  via e-mail, text, or phone and will return every call within twenty-
  four hours. This gives you the opportunity to think about what
  you're going to say.

- Time charges—If clients are going to be running around on the
  Web, looking for stuff constantly, that's fine. But they must know
  that any time they phone to tell you something or e-mail you
  about something—basically anytime they ask you to deal with the
  issues—they are going to be charged for time.

- Out of office—You are entitled to a vacation, so when that time
  comes, communicate that you will not be answering phones or
  returning phone calls for a certain period of time.

Of course, there will always be an occasional client who breaks the
rules. If clients blast you about improperly handling a phone call, reference your communication guide. If they complain about a time charge,
reference your communication guide. If a client becomes verbally abusive
or threatens to fire you if you don't return a call within an hour, perhaps
it's time you fired that client.

The Client Budget

We know budgeting is an issue some designers would rather not get involved in, but we think it helps if the designer creates the budget. Certainly, every project and every client is different, but there are a lot of common questions that can be answered during budgeting. It behooves you to become familiar with the client budgeting process.

The most important question is: How much does the client want to budget for the project? Wouldn't it be wonderful if clients actually had an idea of how much things cost? Most clients generally don't have a clue, nor do they know how to come up with a "realistic" budget. If you truly want to control all of your projects, jump in and offer to help your "spreadsheet-challenged" clientele put theirs together.

The Preliminary Budget

At minimum, the designer needs to handle the preliminary budget. This requires you to think about what the project should look like and how the client's tastes will translate into home furnishings, accessories, textiles, etc. The idea is to work out how much you feel should be applied to each item needed to complete the project (for example, carpet cost: $XXX; sofa cost: $XXX; drapery cost: $XXX; etc.).

By being presented with some sort of figure, the client is allowed to react and ask questions. Then, together, you and the client can finalize the budget numbers. (Note: being masters of our domain and the presented price, we add 15 percent to the total budget for items that clients insist be added because they simply can't live without them.)

If you want an example of how our "no-frills" budgeting works in the real world, recently, a client who was remodeling a home asked us to work up a budget based on a series of discussions we had. The client had already paid a design fee, and we were underway with preliminary selections. As far as budgeting the project, we first leveraged our network. A builder we suggested came up with a budget for all the items we wanted to do in the remodel. The whole thing was extensive; the remodel budget for a 3,500-square-foot home came in at over $400,000. After crunching (and then using) the builder's estimates, we started working on the interior budget.

We built a spreadsheet, breaking the entire space down room by room, adding the individual prices of all the selected items we wanted to install as line items. We knew we were going to purchase most line items, but we also included items we might purchase.

Tier Your Budget Proposals

From the interior budget, we expanded to a preliminary budget that was inclusive of all costs: interiors, exteriors, and otherwise. We always make sure to tier all of our preliminary budget proposals so that clients have the benefit of choosing from a range of pricing options (from lowest price, to a middle option, to top-of-the-line).

In this instance, the variation between the highest and lowest estimates came to around $150,000. The client selected the middle price, and we were happy to move forward. We charged the client time for the hours we spent working. That client understood the fees and had no problem with us helping to create the budget. Everyone was happy. See, that wasn't so hard, was it?

NINE RULES OF CLIENT ENGAGEMENT

After a client signs off on your firm's communication and project guidelines as well as your budget, you are officially off and running. Look at you go! We're so proud; now don't trip. We wish we could give you a road map to the finish line, but there is no one uniform route to managing clients while on your journey.

That said, there are a few common landmines you should be aware of before you go sprinting across uncharted territory. If you want to hydrate your business mind before you get all worked up, try soaking in our Nine Divine Rules of Client Engagement below, and then see if you can avoid the pitfalls that have made many promising design firms pull up lame.

1. Never Do Favors

Here's a biggie: Design firms should never "do favors." If you do, the client will never recognize that a favor has been done. By that, we mean it's okay to bill a client for an item (or time) and then show a 100-percent reduction in price on the invoice, but you should never just write something off without recording it in your paper trail.

If you are giving a client a 100-percent price reduction, for whatever reason, be sure to mail the invoice to the client. By disclosing the actual cost to clients, they become very much aware of what your firm has done to show appreciation for their continued support. If you simply don't bill, they will never know you did them a favor. Always put the "favor" in writing.

2. Avoid Window Shoppers

Beware of window shoppers, those people who feign serious interest in your services but really are wasting your time. It is almost a universal rule that as a young designer, you will be approached by scores of window shoppers who think they can take advantage of your naïveté. Here are some of their common tricks:

- Window shoppers love to blow into a design studio, ask for free design advice or help in sourcing a piece of furniture or a fabric, and then leave without saying so much as "thank you."

- Window shoppers love to ask young designers to make huge presentations, only to say, "How much? Are you crazy? Goodbye!"

Be mindful of these wolves in sheep's clothing. They are efficiency killers who distract you from your real clients. Discriminate and use common sense. Remember, you aren't maintaining a library for the benefit of the public. That's why designers charge for presentations.

3. Guard Your Intellectual Property

A variation on the window-shopping client is a person who steals your design schemes. An altogether nasty lot, these sneaks feign serious interest in a designer, requesting a presentation and courting ceremony, only to turn them down cold while stealing their ideas. It's a cruel world out there; that's why we ask for a retainer before any official presentation.

Your design-ideas are valuable intellectual property, so protect what's upstairs at all times. Never ever give away free advice. It will do nothing to advance your career and will only attract other bloodsuckers.

Once, a friend of a friend took us for a ride. She actually got us all the way up to her house and then, when she saw our presentation, said, "Can I keep it overnight to show my husband?" Since she was the friend of a friend, we made an exception. The next day, she returned our presentation and said, "No, none of it worked—sorry!" In the end, we heard reports that it worked out very well for her. She stole our ideas and found someone else to do it.

4. Don't Be a Marriage Counselor

Do not get stuck being a marriage counselor, a priest, or a psychiatrist for any of your clients. When you are working on a home for a couple, only deal with one spokesperson, not two. With only one client contact point, chances of getting in the middle of a sticky domestic situation are decreased.

Once we worked with a couple who fought like Taylor and Burton throughout their entire project. The husband constantly wanted one thing while the wife wanted another. She even had the gall to ask us to intervene on her behalf in order to convince the hubby of her way of doing it. We begrudgingly accepted, voicing her concerns to her husband as if we had thought of them ourselves. But we felt uncomfortable and decided to never involve ourselves in a War of the Roses–type situation again. We say, Leave the counseling for counselors and stay away from dysfunctional clients.

5. Do Not Get Personal

It is absolutely inappropriate to get personal with clients. No one can talk design business over cocktails and dinner. If you ask us, pathological socialization with clients is a big-time mistake. Our motto goes like this: Go in, do the work, then get the hell out. But what if the client wants to get friendly? Isn't a fancy meal out at a nice restaurant a perk? Sure, but do make sure it is after the project has been completed. Until the project is up and running, you don't go to dinner.

Clients have to understand that you are a professional. Take whatever precautions are necessary, but guard your privacy and don't get personal. We used to let clients call us on Sundays, and what a can of worms that opened up. It didn't take long for us to change our tune and our home phone number. Only give out your *business* number to clients. Remember, designers: it's show business, not show friendship.

6. Stay Inspired with Boring Clients

Here is a reality check. Not every project will make banner headlines, not every client is a rock star, and not every project will grace the cover of a shelter magazine. Stay inspired even when you work with "boring" clients who have no sizzle, style, or inspiration by getting inspired by the project itself. You're doing what you love. Even if you do a job and there is no real connection with the client, stay focused and energetic and get turned on by the business side of things.

For all of you aspiring luxury residential designers, you are also going to have to contend with the "curse of the bourgeoisie," which means clients who are decorating their third or fourth home. Having already decorated three mansions, your filthy rich clients may not have much energy left for your design process. You may hear things like, "Oh, this is fabulous, yawn." Again, who cares? As long as you're making money, that should be inspiration enough.

7. Don't Wield a Heavy Sales Hand

Once you have gotten in the good graces of your clients, don't continually lay heavy sell jobs on them, insisting that they expand their project or purchase goods that are too expensive for their budget. If a client hires you for a small project, leave it at that. If clients are looking for more work to be done, they will come back to you. If you lay off and give them some breathing room, it may be a common occurrence for clients to approach you in the middle of a small project and say, "After we finish this room, why don't we look at this or that?"

This is an outrageous example, but let's say you are renovating a client's kitchen and bath, and you notice a television sitting on the floor in the living room. While you work on his kitchen, casually let him know that you also create and install built-ins for home entertainment systems. Then, tell him, "When you want it done, come see us; we won't pressure you." It gives the client the feeling that he is in control.

8. Follow Up with a Smile

What about the designer who has a client who is still "sitting on the fence"? If you have extended an LOA and heard chirping crickets in return, we suggest you follow up with that client *one* time. No more. Trust us, if the client is truly interested, he or she will pull the trigger almost right away. If not, there may be other problems of which you are unaware that could ultimately impact your profit margin. The client's hesitation may turn out to be a blessing.

If you're determined to land the fence-sitting client, try following up a month later with a photo postcard of one of your installations. Include a note on the back saying something about the pictured project and how the client loved the results. Avoid making reference to the LOA.

9. Bless It and Move On

If you are ever presented with a potential litigation scenario, talk to your lawyer and find out what it is ultimately going to cost you. Ask yourself if you'd rather be right or happy. We had an experience in which we fought with a client in small-claims court when we really should have just paid the fee and moved on.

Understand what you can do and what you can't. Leave vengeance for the universe. If all you're doing is generating negative energy, you have no idea where it will come back to haunt you. Try adopting our little motto: If you can't change it, you have to bless it and move on. If that ship has sailed, it's sailed. Mind the gap! Move on and do your business.

KISS THE BUMS GOODBYE

Sometimes, it's advisable to let a client walk rather than suffer the slings, arrows, and nasty words that come with an unhappy being. We've found it rare to have to "fire" a client, but it does happen. You want to be very careful about which clients you fire and for what reasons. There are always the questions of fees that may have to be returned and whether or not deposits are returnable. Once the decision has been made, the best thing is to move as quickly as possible to close the transaction with the offending client.

Once, we had a client who became verbally abusive. We weren't sleeping and worried all the time about the situation. We kept putting that client off until the person finally demanded we return the money. We had over $20,000 in deposits from the client, and were owed in excess of $10,000 in delivered goods. We also had time charges against our retainer, which amounted to the total retainer.

What a mess, right? This is what happens when you have to fire a client mid-stream. It is like a designer divorce, but hopefully, your attorney is left out of it. In the above case, it took some time to resolve the situation, but in the end, we settled out of court and made a 42 percent profit. We were thrilled to "kiss the bums goodbye" and point our firm toward a better tomorrow.

PLOTTING A GAME PLAN FOR YOUR BUSINESS

Of all the lessons we have accorded you on this long, strange trip through the design forest, which do you think is the one a young entrepreneur must embody at all times? If you said professionalism, by Jove, we think you've finally got it. Not to pummel a dead horse, but we want to spend these final precious hours of our business practices boot camp going over a few more ways you can professionally game-plan the running of a sole-proprietor business so that you're making the most of your talent and wonderful new job opportunities on day one.

Pay Yourself a Salary

Seeing as you're on the threshold of billing clients, you need to make sure you set up your books so you're paid for your efforts. It's important that every design entrepreneur pay him- or herself some form of salary.

We know you are the boss, but paying yourself a salary is symbolic. We don't pay ourselves a big salary, but we still do it. Why? It helps to psychologically separate the designer from the business and creates the feeling that what you are doing is not a hobby. Playing these little mind games is just another tool for helping you understand that design is a job just like any other, and the business owner (in this case, you) needs to pay every employee.

We know it will be tempting, but resist the urge to leave as much money in your business coffer as possible. While it's true that your business needs as much cash flow as it can get, you also must recognize the value of your own services. Paying yourself a salary does that.

Make Business Travel Profitable

Once you begin networking, you'll meet decorators who love to regale the world with glamorous stories about their latest buying trip. "Buying trip" is a term thrown around liberally these days; it can mean merely a day trip to the nearest metropolitan city to source or purchase goods or services, or it can mean an international trip abroad (to, say, Paris or Argentina) to purchase rare luxury goods.

The purpose of making a trip depends on whether your intention is to stock inventory or to supply a need for a client. Some buying trips may even be "look-see" trips with no purchases at the time. Even though all three options sound like loads of fun, time is money, so make sure your buying trips are profitable.

Ultimately, the amount you charge for the items you purchase must be less than the amount you spend on the trip. Determine how much the trip costs in terms of time out of the office and expenses.

For us, a day trip to San Francisco is low-cost and usually high-return. These days, we travel not to stock inventory but to source fabrics, furniture, and accessories for individual jobs. With the time we are out of the office and the cost of fuel, parking, lunch, etc., we still manage to make a profit while quickly and efficiently sourcing the items we need for a client.

Long-distance travel, whether to another city or abroad, brings with it another whole set of challenges, like the cost of shipping, exchange rates, and the like. It is not for the faint of heart. Something else to consider is the office hours it will take to locate sources in the destination city, arrange for meetings and showings, etc. All prep work must take place before you leave for the trip.

Despite what you hear, an international trip really isn't all that glamorous. A designer should not be blinded by first-class airfare. It is still work and should be treated just like any other part of the job. We prefer the client not to come along on buying trips, but there are occasions when it's just the ticket, so to speak. In those instances, if an eager client is on hand to cover all out-of-pocket expenses as well as make on-the-spot decisions regarding purchases, all the better. (We always insist on separate accommodations when you travel with clients, however, as the last thing a designer wants is to be onstage twenty-four hours a day.)

How do you charge for travel? In traveling for a client, the tendency is to charge less hourly because of the large number of hours involved, especially in traveling overnight or on multiple overnight trips. We reduce our rate for extended travel time, since it is almost impossible to rationalize normal hourly billing when you are spending time in your hotel after hours.

Remember, when you are presenting your travel estimate, success is predicated on being completely open with the client. Start by explaining your point of view. If the designer is a sole proprietor, there is the question of missed opportunities at the office if he or she is away for an extended period. In addition, who will oversee the operation until the principal returns if he or she has a limited staff? If you are living right, these concerns might be offset by payment from the client. If not, it probably wasn't worth your time in the first place.

Here are the terms we request from clients before we make a commitment to travel:

- Cost of airfare: business, or first-class if the trip is longer than three hours
- Separate hotel accommodations
- Meals and taxi/car rental expenses
- An hourly fee

Strategize to Fill Containers

A container is a shipping module primarily used for intercontinental shipments. The size of shipping containers is quoted in cubic feet and is priced that way. One of the most profitable ways to maximize the use of a container is to fill every crevice. That means that if you have a buffet, for example, fill the inside with smaller items that will fit inside. The same goes for the whole container.

Often, a designer is able to share a container with other people shipping things to the same general area. There are consolidators in most large cities in Asia and Europe, in particular, who deal solely in multiple users of the same container. Cost, of course, is based on the way the container is shipped, with shipment by sea being the most affordable. Airfreight can be very expensive.

CASE STUDY: A WEEKEND IN THE COUNTRY

One time I (Robert) was invited to Maine by a client to work on her summer home. I flew up on a Thursday and planned to return on Sunday afternoon. I had agreed on a day rate for the time I would be out of the office, and my expenses would be paid. I thought, What could go wrong? The answer: everything.

I won't go into details, but upon my arrival, I realized, to my horror, that I was there for the client's entertainment. I had hardly gotten seated in the car when the design questions started. They didn't stop the entire weekend. What had I gotten myself into? These people sucked free advice from me nonstop all weekend, and they didn't even provide lively conversation or good company! They were plain boring, and I was plain bored by the end of the weekend.

Once I returned to the office, we reassessed our travel procedures. As a result, we now insist our accommodations be a small hotel or bed and breakfast. That way, we can get away every evening. We also try, as often as possible, to limit out-of-town work to one business day during the week. No weekends. We know it's not always possible, but we certainly try.

We have even flown round-trip from Baltimore to St. Paul in the same day! It was a long day, yes, but also very profitable. And we didn't have to tap-dance onstage for days on end.

MANAGING YOUR MONEY

Once your income starts coming in, you need to insure proper management and disbursement of it all. Yes, there are going to be rules for you to learn and concepts to absorb. The idea here is to make sure you put your income where it will do the most good. It is, after all, a business, and you want to be profitable.

If you haven't gathered this by now, all design firms set their own unique retail price for goods and services. Yours should be based on how much you pay for a given product and what percentage point you need to mark it up to profit from the exchange. It doesn't matter what the manufacturer suggests "should" be the retail price; it is the job of the individual design firm to arrive at a percentage that works for them. It will be a sorry day if professional organizations ever try to take away this basic freedom. Such regulation would make us feel like we were trying to run a design business in Communist China. We hope to never live to see that day, but it unfortunately might come.

Devise a Markup Formula

The best way to determine your markup formula is to look at your overhead. Then, decide how much is needed on each sale to succeed with a reasonable margin of profit. Most designers tend to undervalue goods, so don't be afraid to charge more if it is appropriate.

We use a markup between 2.35 and 2.45 times the original cost. The higher markup percentage is for lower-priced goods that don't generate large income. The smaller percentage is for items like furniture, drapery, etc. that are "higher cost" and will naturally return a larger profit. This markup includes all packing, freight, delivery, and overhead costs.

Grow with Cash Flow

Be diligent about monitoring your firm's financial strength. Keep constant tabs on your company cash flow. If at all possible, we suggest that designers maintain enough liquid cash in their business account to cover three months' expenses. We know that's easier said than done, but you simply must try.

Maintaining ample liquidity is a great practice for a young business because it gives you flexibility to evolve. Much like planting a seed in a large pot where it can take root and grow, cash flow is like fertile soil for your design visions. Whether it's having the money to add a new profit arm (like a product line) or taking advantage of a killer discount (like someone selling inventory at a fire-sale price), it makes sense for you to stay financially nimble if you want to nourish a healthy, prosperous business.

Have Comfort in Reserve

In addition to ample cash flow, an emergency reserve is another great indicator of a firm's strength. Twenty years ago, we didn't have the same wherewithal we do today. Now, we have a reserve that will pay for an additional twelve months of business expenses if we run into an extended dry spell. We aren't talking about borrowing from your 401(k) or Roth IRA; we mean a cash reserve (in a high-yield money market account) that's just for the business.

Ideally, you want enough "rainy day" money to last an entire year, but that may not be realistic for many young entrepreneurs. Still, do the best you can while knowing that interior design is a cyclical business. The most successful designers make a practice of socking away nuts like squirrels to prepare for winter. Understand the cycles in your region; then, when you're cooking (i.e., flush with clients and money), start socking away money in your emergency reserve. Odds are, at some point, you're going to need it.

Estimate Income Needs

Since we're on the topic of cash flow, let's talk about your income needs. Will your client projects actually bring in enough money to pay your bills? The best way to estimate your income is simple. Make some sort of SWAG (sophisticated wild-a– guess) as to how much total income you expect to make during the first year of business. Then, deduct the fixed costs of the business like rent, electric, phone, salaries, insurance, etc. Also, deduct the total projected cost for all the goods you sell clients.

This will leave you with a gross net amount, which is your profit or the money you get to keep. There will be a few other expenses (taxes and the like), but nevertheless, this exercise will give you a pretty good idea of how much you will make the first year. Now, ask yourself:

- Is that amount enough to satisfy my lifestyle?
- If not, can I do more business?
- Can I add another profit arm?
- Should I raise my rates?

Remember, by adding 5 percent to each retail price, you will see 5 percent more income for your gross net. It's amazing how it all comes down to a little simple adding, subtracting, and multiplying, isn't it?

Determine How Many Hours You Must Bill

If you are able to make a SWAG estimate of your total income, then you probably have a goal for how much you want to earn annually from this business venture. Now, wouldn't it be great if you knew how many hours you need to bill each year to meet your goal? You actually can figure it out by working backwards.

Say you want to walk away from your business with $50,000 every year and make your money charging design fees with time billed against retainers. How many hours will you have to charge to make $50,000 clear? First, making $50,000 (after the cost of goods) isn't nearly enough, as a significant portion of your total income goes toward paying your business overhead (i.e., fixed costs). So, let's say you need to make $75,000 annually (to cover all overhead) in order to net you out at $50,000. Let's also say you charge $100 per hour. You have to bill 750 hours annually. That may sound like a lot, but you only have to bill fifteen hours per week to get there.

If you realize that you are not going to be able to pay your overhead or clear enough net profit to satisfy your lifestyle, you may want to consider raising your rates right now. Believe us, it happens all the time. Even designers who use transparent pricing are raising their rates by 3 to 4 percent annually. Remember, those few percentage points go directly to the bottom line. So, what are you charging? Is it enough?

In the end, so many designers are not focused on reality when they really must be. Every business has to make money or it will cease to exist. That's not to say that you, as the designer, must make money, but you have to be able to make enough to sustain your business costs, staff, bills, etc. or you are sunk. If you take the few extra steps described above and actually game-plan your financial year, you will be better prepared mentally to meet all of your financial goals.

Evaluate Your Success

Every quarter, young entrepreneurs should stop to evaluate how their business is doing. Ask yourself questions like:

- Philosophically, where are we going?
- Financially, how are we doing?
- Are we on track to meet our annual goals?

Although we constantly assess and reassess our business, forecasting is still difficult—particularly in the design industry.

If you'd like feedback on how you manage clients, try taking a few to lunch (after their projects are complete, of course) and ask them about their experience. What did you do right? What could have been done better? This process is all about continuing your education.

Here are a few more areas in which you can evaluate your business:

- Your team—Do you have a strong back-up staff to make your projects flow? Do the other designers in your firm also bring in business, or are you the only rainmaker? Look at your employees' performance evaluations to see who is pulling his or her own weight. Your clientele—Evaluate the quality of your clientele. Are you where you want to be in terms of your ideal target market?

- Your projects—Do your projects continue to get larger over time? Hopefully, they do. Your designs—Is your creativity on par with your client's expectations? Can you hone your skills to get better?

- Your service—Are your clients pleased with the way you operate? Is there good follow-up with vendors and clients?

- Your office—Is the office run in a professional way? Are you maximizing your office time?

- Your cash flow—Are you billing enough time to meet your annual goals? Do you need to raise rates or cut down on overhead?

- Your marketing—Are you putting yourself out there? Are you fostering new industry relationships while you are fabulously visible in the design world? Are you getting published?

CASE STUDY: MARK CUTLER DESIGN, INC

We would like to give one of the final words in our paperback symposium to a good guy in the design world, the talented celebrity designer Mark Cutler. For those of you who missed his show on A&E, Mark is the president of Mark Cutler Design, Inc., an interior design firm based in Los Angeles, California.

He was named one of the Top Forty Designers in America by the *Robb Report* and is a good friend of Hale-Williams Interiors. Mark was gracious enough to stop by our designer kitchen to give you a few final pointers. Take it away, Mark.

Success

I'm happy to get one of the last words in your mentor series. I have a lot of time for Tom and Robert because they seem like people I can trust and the purity of their intention is clear. I have always been impressed with their openness to sharing their experience and, probably more importantly, their openness to listening to other people's ideas, weighing them against what they already know, and making a sound decision. It is no surprise that this book puts them in the mentor role. I think that alone speaks volumes about their character.

As for my career, I appreciate Hale-Williams saying I'm a star, but I'm not sure that's the case. I have great respect for tradition, and it's important for me to see my work as a continuation of all that has come before me. That's why I'm here to give you a few tips on how to make it in this business, even if you are picking up the practice as an altogether new vocation.

I wish I could say my company is the result of a grand plan. As I suspect was the case with a lot of you, my getting into the field was really more of an accident than anything else. Once I dove in, I immediately developed a strategy for what I thought was success. I always felt that, since I was coming to the profession a little later than most, I had a lot of catching up to do. I'd like to share tips from the strategies I followed early in my career to build my firm.

Catch-up Strategy Tips

Take every project that comes your way. Small, medium, or large—in the beginning, it doesn't matter. Of course, this may mean working seven days a week, but I believe you need to develop a body of work as quickly as possible. If you are a late bloomer, like me, you should take every project you can.

Take projects at a cut rate. Consider cutting your rates if you think a particular project may become a "banner project" for your portfolio, Web site, or the press. Think about taking jobs solely because a client is well-connected and may be a source of future referrals. For example, a few years ago, when one of my ex-employees decided to get married, I decided to design her new house gratis. I did it because I wanted to thank her for all the years of service, but in addition, I felt that the home could be a great "banner project." Yes, my former assistant married well. As it turns out, the house was ultimately published in four different magazines and she has referred many clients to me over the years. (I am currently working on a third residence for her and her husband.)

Market your business to a younger clientele. This is smart, especially in the beginning, because these clients still have two or three more houses in their future. As Tom and Robert say, "These are your people, so go to them."

One thing to keep in mind in working with clients is that you are dealing with people's dreams. It's not just their home; it's how they present themselves to the world. It's the place where they will raise their children. That's a big deal, and one I take very seriously. Never get in the way of your client; your job is to create a home that is a portrait of the client and not a vehicle for your ego.

And finally, here are some catch-up tips for marketing:

- *Foster ties within the community—Develop relationships with showrooms, vendors, and other designers. There are a lot of petty people in this industry who jealously guard their turf. I think that time is coming to an end.*

- *Be open about how you do business—I firmly believe that the success of those around me will bring success to me, as well. A rising tide raises all boats.*

- *Embrace a proactive PR campaign—I've worked with a publicist now for several years in an effort to create a strong public profile through appearances in the media. This has included having projects published, getting quoted, having a blog, etc. I even had my own TV show on A&E for a few seasons. Creating a strong message and public persona is extremely important; it gives you instant credibility and differentiates you from your competitors.*

- *Create a unified message—I work with my staff to create a unified message so that there is a unity to the outreach that we do.*

- *Do charitable work—It's important that you become an active member of a community and are held responsible for taking an active role. What we do as designers is all about creating a lifestyle, so it is important that we set an example of how it can be done with integrity and virtue.*

PREPARING THE UNPREPARED

During our numerous years in the industry, we've met scores of young people, mostly young women, who are interested in becoming design entrepreneurs, yet have no clue regarding how to run a business. In our wisdom, we've found that most aspiring designers have trouble talking about money matters. It has gotten so bad today that it's become an epidemic.

After seeing how ill-prepared some young designers are to face the rigors of the real world, it finally became a passion of ours to find a way to help ensure that these students succeed in their chosen field. So, we decided to teach, lecture, and (oh, yes) write a book about the business of interior design.

Has some of our passion for the "business" been contagious? Can you now see what a shame it is that your university didn't recognize design as a profession worthy of a real business education? By now, we certainly hope so. We also hope that with a better idea of how our industry works, you don't make the same mistake as our mortarboard-wearing brethren. Never lose sight of the fact that design is a business, not an art.

The First Step Is the Hardest Part

When it comes to your entrepreneurial career, sometimes the hardest part is actually deciding to open a business. Once you are over that hurdle, the work begins, and it tends to become easier to focus on the tasks at hand. Your first year in business will likely be very trying, but it will tell you a lot about how you handle the stress of, for instance, not having a regular paycheck or the multi tasking involved in making your business run properly.

Your stamina and ability to roll with the punches will be tested. A lot of external factors may affect your success ratio (i.e., how "new business" comes in and whether or not expenses can be paid), but let's not minimize the fact that simply surviving your first year should be a particular moment for celebration! Survival means that you live to fight another day and have met and conquered many of the challenges that have slain lesser designers. That is a wonderful thing.

Sometimes You Need a Kick Start

Unfortunately, even surviving the first year doesn't mean your company is out of the woods. The challenges will go on and on. We, for instance, still face challenges every day after all this time in the business. When you run into rough patches, don't be afraid to take chances. Be bold enough to stand out, if that's what you're really all about.

Reinvent your business model, add to your design services, find a partner—innovate, and do it like no other designer you know. Have you noticed that everyone tries to be the best at what they do? Well, why not try to be the *only* one who does what you do?

Evolve Your Brand (Like Us)

There may be times when we all have to take a step back and kick-start our brand image or business plan. Even successful designers must learn to reinvent themselves and evolve with the sign of the times. That is part of positioning.

If you are dubious, take a look at what we have done. At Hale-Williams, we have evolved our brand simply by writing this book. Not only that, but if you go back and review the lesson plan, you will see that we followed our blueprint for success to a tee. By writing about the business of interior design, we:

- Evolved our brand image to include mentoring
- Further established ourselves as experts in the field
- Created another profit arm for the business
- Set ourselves apart from the pack
- Added another layer to our marketing efforts

How to Improve Your Game after Year One

There are many ways to improve your game after your first year in business. Here are some suggestions that we have for you after you reach that milestone:

- Increase your fees by at least 10 percent.
- Divest yourself of some of the day-to-day items you must do that interfere with getting out there and selling your services.
- Hire a purchasing firm, a part-time bookkeeper, or an office manager to free up time for you to create.
- Become more involved with a professional group, community group, or industry discussion group in your area.
- Create a design blog or write about decorating for a local newspaper.
- Position yourself locally as a successful professional who is the "go-to" guy or gal for information on the design industry.
- Attend one national industry event in a city outside of yours. This will give you a new perspective on the business as well as a little time out of the office. Treat the trip as a reward for a job well done.

You see, it's not so hard to evolve if you put your mind to it. Just realize that once you think you've got it all figured out, you probably don't. Things change, the industry changes, and over time, your audience will change, too. As one gains experience, one's audience becomes older and more affluent.

Your ability to evolve is all part of the business. No matter what model you adopt or which segment you dive into, change is just around the corner. You will change, the world will change, your competition will change, and you must, in turn, change with them.

Now It's Time to Execute

Once you get out into the real world, you will realize that most designers at cocktail parties still want to talk about "decorating" instead of "the business," so we hope you have enjoyed your time with your old mentors. Guys like us don't come around every day!

If not now, we hope that one day soon, you will truly appreciate what we do and value the lessons we have shared. Business practices may not be glamorous, but if you take heed and execute like a professional, they will make a lasting difference in your professional life.

More than anything, we want some young designer to come up to us one day after reading this book and say, "Gosh, I never thought I could do it, but you have given me the inspiration to go out there and give it a try." That would be simply divine.

AFTERWORD

We certainly hope our journey through the intricacies of the business of interior design has helped you gain insight into an industry that is both competitive and wonderfully fulfilling. It will take a tremendous amount of courage to create your business. It won't be easy, and you will not see instant success. Many of you will not see yourselves as talented, courageous entrepreneurs, but simply as people looking to make a living. Then, one day you will turn around and look back over the past year or two, and you will wonder where the time has gone. You won't wonder how you could have spent that time, because you will be too busy congratulating yourself on your ability to own and operate a successful interior design business. With your work will come a grand sense of accomplishment. There aren't a lot of people who have the ability to create a dream and bring it to fruition.

We've given you the fundamentals. You've studied the various design segments, built your business plan, researched your target market, and opened your design studio. Along the way, you've learned how to write contracts and letters of agreement, market yourself, prepare creative and succinct presentations, and develop a network of business allies. You now understand how to manage your clients and budget for them and your business; you have a firm grasp of pricing and fees and how they impact your business model. As we said in the beginning, becoming an entrepreneurial interior designer is not easy. It requires both a strong grounding in the basics of interior design and an understanding of the principles of business practice. You have to want this more than anything you've ever wanted in your life. It requires tenacity and an unflagging desire to prevail. You will be creating a chance to achieve your destiny.

Keeping the dream alive will also become a part of your life. Meeting and working with other like-minded interior designers will help reinvigorate your passion. As we close, we are preparing to attend the fifth annual

Business of Design conference in Las Vegas. This conference has been one of the most enlightening events of our professional life. We surround ourselves with over three hundred interior designers from all parts of the United States and spend all our time talking about the business of interior design. Like all of you, the group is a wonderful mélange of residential and commercial interior designers, as well as those people interested in the business. We attend a conference like this to increase our ability to prevail in a business that has changed over the years and will continue to change. We are bombarded with new ideas at every turn, and we will continue to assess those ideas and incorporate into our business model methods that will increase our effectiveness as designers and businesspeople.

This book, for us, has been a rewarding and challenging journey. So is our business. We both wish each and every one of you the best of luck in finding your particular niche in the profession and becoming the very best you can be within your arena.

INDEX

Books from Allworth Press

Allworth Press is an imprint of Allworth Communications, Inc. Selected titles are listed below.

The Challenge of Interior Design: Professional Values and Opportunities
by Mary V. Knackstedt (*paperback, 6 × 9, 272 pages, $24.95*)

How to Start and Operate Your Own Design Firm: A Guide for Interior Designers and Architects, Second Edition
by Albert W. Rubeling, Jr., FAIA (*paperback, 6 × 9, 256 pages, $24.95*)

Business and Legal Forms for Interior Designers
by Tad Crawford and Eva Doman Bruck (*paperback, 8 ½ × 11, 240 pages, $29.95*)

The Interior Designer's Guide to Pricing, Estimating, and Budgeting
by Theo Stephan Williams (*paperback, 6 × 9, 208 pages, $19.95*)

How to Think Like a Great Graphic Designer
by Debbie Millman (*paperback, 6 × 9, 248 pages, $24.95*)

The Graphic Designer's Guide to Better Business Writing
by Barbara Janoff and Ruth Cash-Smith (*paperback, 6 × 9, 256 pages, $19.95*)

Creating the Perfect Design Brief: How to Manage Design for Strategic Advantage
by Peter L. Phillips (*paperback, 6 × 9, 224 pages, $19.95*)

The Graphic Design Business Book
by Tad Crawford (*paperback, 6 × 9, 256 pages, $24.95*)

Graphic Designer's Guide to Clients: How to Make Clients Happy and Do Great Work
by Ellen Shapiro (*paperback, 6 × 9, 256 pages, $19.95*)

AIGA Professional Practices in Graphic Design, Second Edition
edited by Tad Crawford (*paperback, 6 × 9, 336 pages, $29.95*)

Designing Logos: The Process of Creating Logos That Endure
by Jack Gernsheimer (*paperback, 8 ½ × 10, 208 pages, $35.00*)

Designing Effective Communications: Creating Contexts for Clarity and Meaning
edited by Jorge Frascara (*paperback, 6 × 9, 304 pages, 100 b&w illustrations, $24.95*)

To request a free catalog or order books by credit card, call 1-800-491-2808. To see our complete catalog on the World Wide Web, or to order online for a 20 percent discount, you can find us at ***www.allworth.com.***